THE GREAT COOKS' GUIDE TO

Clay
Cookery

America's leading food authorities share their home-tested
recipes and expertise on cooking equipment and techniques

THE GREAT COOKS' GUIDE TO

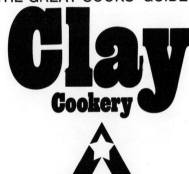

Clay
Cookery

A BEARD GLASER WOLF BOOK

RANDOM HOUSE, NEW YORK

Book Design by Milton Glaser, Inc.

Cover Photograph by Richard Jeffery

Library of Congress Cataloguing in Publication Data

Main entry under title:

The Great cooks' guide to clay cookery.

(The Great cooks' library)
1. Clay pot cookery. 2. Kitchen utensils.
I. Title: Clay cookery. II. Series.
TX825.5.G73   641.5'88   77-5970
ISBN 0-394-73420-3

Manufactured in the United States of America
2 4 6 8 9 7 5 3
First Edition

We have gathered together some of the great cooks in this country to share their recipes—and their expertise—with you. As you read the recipes, you will find that in certain cases techniques will vary. That is as it should be: cooking is a highly individual art, and our experts have arrived at their own personal methods through years of experience in the kitchen.

THE EDITORS

Contents

MEATS

DESSERTS

*Cookery made great progress
when fire-resisting vessels in
bronze or clay appeared.*

J. A. Brillat-Savarin

Clay Cookery

More and more, we are simplifying the way we live. As the world around us becomes increasingly frantic, we are turning our attention more and more to the basic values that gave meaning to our great-grandparents' lives. Not that we are eager to chop wood, split kindling and fan life into a wood-burning stove instead of flicking on the gas or electricity! Those tasks were never much fun. But we do want the hearty, earthy food those stoves produced: braised beef free of rich sauces, sweet and succulent corn-on-the-cob needing only a dab of butter, and moist, savory roast chicken surrounded by carrots and onions.

We can have that wholesome and flavorful food today. We skip the wood-burning stove and its attendant drudgery, and go back to a method older than civilization itself—cooking in wet clay. By accident, or by a leap of genius, some Neolithic hunter discovered that game could be daubed with wet clay from a river bank, then placed in the smoldering coals of a fire to cook. This method, in contrast to holding meat over a flame, left in the juices and did not require constant attention. As the clay hardened, the meat was sealed in a protective casing where it cooked slowly, basted in its own juices. It lost none of its savor, and became as tender as sinewy wild game ever could. If you'd like to try this method (for a bird that's guaranteed to be tender), one of our great cooks has provided a recipe for Chinese chicken baked in a clay robe. It's not an everyday meal perhaps, but one sure to delight and amuse your guests.

Clay-wrapping was the beginning of the one-pot meal. Unfortunately, it was also a one-meal pot; to get at the meat, the cavemen diners had to break the clay covering. This may have been all right for hunters on the march with no dish-washing worries, but civilized folk wanted more permanent cooking vessels. Over twenty centuries ago, the Etruscans, luxury-loving neighbors of the early Romans, devised such a pot. They were master-workers in terra-cotta—that is, porous, unglazed, fired clay. Terra-cotta statues graced their magnificent temples, and terra-cotta cookware stood in the kitchens of their splendid villas. The Romans eventually destroyed the Etruscan civilization, but not before they had adopted their clay cooking pots. The Romans knew a good thing when they saw it!

How Wet Clay Works: Now wet clay cooking is enjoying a renaissance. Don't confuse wet-clay cookers with glazed earthenware cooking pots, which have a venerable history all their own. Once a pot is glazed it is no longer porous; that is, it cannot absorb water. The pots we are talking about are purposely left unglazed, at least in part, like so many flower pots, so that they can soak up a considerable amount of water. The principle of wet clay cooking is this: porous clay allows some vapors to escape, so that a great deal of liquid does not accumulate in the cooker. As the wet clay dries, evaporating water bathes the food in a light cloud of steam so that it does not stick to the pot. Food cooks with a minimum of liquid and no additional fat. All nutrients remain in the pot, a boon to dieters and the health-conscious alike.

The best-known modern versions of the unglazed clay pot are imported from Germany—the Römertopf (literally, "Roman Pot") and Schlemmertopf (roughly, "feast pot"). Both body and lid of the Römertopf are completely unglazed, inside and out, with a ridged bottom to elevate a roast or chicken slightly so that it is bathed in savory vapor and browns on all sides. Yes, food does brown in porous clay, even with the lid on! The Schlemmertopf lid is unglazed, but the pot has a slick of glazing inside the bottom to facilitate cleaning. Both brands come in five sizes, from a small pot that's just right for dinner for two, to one big enough to hold the Thanksgiving turkey. There are also British-made clay pots appropriately called "bricks"—chicken bricks, fish bricks, and one made especially for bread-baking. As a guide, we have given the liquid capacity of the bottom half of the pot in which each recipe was tested. However, whatever size pot you have can be used for many of the recipes.

Unlike other cooking vessels, clay pots *must* be soaked before use, for at least fifteen minutes. (If you have any questions, consult the directions that come with your cooker.) The casserole is then filled with food, covered, and placed in a *cold* oven; clay cookers are sturdy, but abrupt changes of temperature may cause them to crack. Turn the heat to the desired temperature, and begin to count cooking time when the oven has reached that heat level. If you want to add liquid to a heated pot, warm it first. Never use the pot over a burner or heating element. Never allow the pot to touch the sides of the oven, and when you remove it from the oven, place it on a folded towel, a cork trivet or a wooden board. Just observe these few precautions, and your pot should serve you well for years.

Clay cookers need a bit of special handling, but their many virtues amply reward you. Once the pot is in the oven, you can more or less forget it until you check for doneness. The food is self-basting; it's almost impossible to burn it. What's more, you can take the pot from the oven and leave it, covered, for up to half an hour—the food will still be warm. Plus, the cookers are attractive enough to go to the table. And the oven stays clean!

Before you use a clay cooker for the first time, immerse the two halves of the pot in water and soak them for half an hour. Then give them a brisk scrub with a stiff brush to remove any traces of brick dust. After that, soak both parts of the cooker for about fifteen minutes before every use.

Cooking Time: If you've never used a clay cooker before, a short run-through of a basic recipe should prove helpful. First, you must keep in mind a rule of thumb for clay-cooking: add 100 degrees to the heat and a half hour to the cooking time specified in most conventional recipes.

Römertopf. Made of unglazed earthenware, the Römertopf must be soaked until thoroughly wet before use. The bottom of the pot is ridged on the inside to prevent food from sticking and to enhance the circulation of steam. Available in five different sizes, the Römertopf also comes with a recipe booklet.

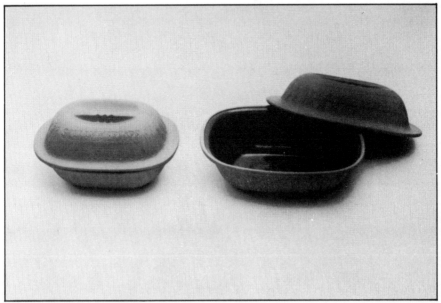

Schlemmertopf. Clay is sometimes hard to clean and will absorb flavors and odors. For easy cleaning, the bottom of the Schlemmertopf is glazed inside. The pot comes in three sizes and shapes — with a recipe booklet.

Chicken Brick. Form follows function in this earthenware pot, specifically designed to embrace a small turkey, large chicken or two small chickens. The porous unglazed brick retains all the moisture and natural flavor of the fowl and has a charm of its own.

Fish Brick. The most attractive way to bake a fish in earthenware is in a specially shaped pot like this one. Unglazed, the porous brick cradles the fish perfectly, enveloping it with steam as it bakes and preserving all its natural juices.

Now, let's take that old stand-by, roast chicken. First, soak the pot while you assemble the ingredients. Rub the chicken with butter for added flavor, if you like; it will roast quite well without it. Salt and pepper it, and put a handful of herbs such as thyme or rosemary in the cavity. Add a quartered onion and a stalk of celery to the pot. Cover, and place it in the center of a cold oven. If a conventional recipe calls for an oven setting of 350 degrees, turn the temperature gauge to 450 degrees. You'll find that even though you're using high heat, the bird takes longer to cook than it does by usual methods. That's because clay will never become as hot as metal. Then begin timing the chicken only when the oven has reached 450 degrees; it usually takes about ten minutes. Thus, if you ordinarily cook a chicken for an hour at 350 degrees, cook it in clay for one and a half hours at 450 degrees. Of course oven and food temperatures vary widely, so while you're still getting to know your cooker, begin to test for doneness thirty minutes early.

The chicken will brown nicely with the lid on; sounds impossible, but it does. However, if you want a very crisp skin, remove the lid for the last fifteen minutes of cooking time. With heavy potholders or barbecue mitts, take the pot from the oven and place it on a folded towel, trivet or board. If you like a gravy with body, you may spoon the juices into a small pan, and thicken them over low heat with a little arrowroot mixed with water, but it isn't necessary. Clay-cooked chicken is so plump, juicy and tender it needs no embellishment.

Cleaning and Care: In cleaning, as in preparation, there are a few vital rules to follow. The first few times you use a clay cooker, you may have to remind yourself of them, but after that they'll be automatic. Once the pot is cool, soak it in warm water with a drop of dishwashing liquid. Sprinkle it with salt and scrub it with a stiff brush or non-metallic abrasive pad. (Don't be tempted to scour it with metal or powders; these would clog the pores and render the pot useless.) When the pot needs a thorough cleaning, soak it in hot water with three tablespoons of baking soda. Clay pots should not go into the dishwasher. Store clean pots uncovered, or with the lids upside down inside them, but never tightly sealed. This gives the pots a chance to dry thoroughly between uses, and eliminates risk of mold.

Because clay is porous, it may retain a suggestion of very strong spices—of chili or curry or saffron—or a vague "fishiness." For this reason many people use separate cookers for fish, meat and desserts. However, experienced cooks on our staff report little or no "hangover." If you have only one clay pot and any doubts about its freshness, give it a long soak in hot water with baking soda. Some cooks prefer to use parchment paper or foil liners—they feel that a liner keeps the pot cleaner and aids in cooking. It's a matter of preference. In any case, don't expect your clay pot to retain the virginal, untouched look it had when you bought it. With use, the pot "seasons" slowly. First, it becomes mottled, then the spots darken and eventually even out as the pot takes on the patina of any well-loved piece of equipment. This is one of the joys of owning an unglazed pot; it acquires its own character and identity. It becomes more beautiful with age.

Soup

HEARTY SOUP FOR A COLD DAY

Isabel S. Cornell

6 to 8 servings

6 TABLESPOONS BULGUR WHEAT (CRACKED WHEAT)
1 POUND LEAN GROUND CHUCK OR ROUND
1 EGG
2 TABLESPOONS SOY SAUCE
1/8 TEASPOON FRESHLY GROUND BLACK PEPPER
2 TABLESPOONS FLOUR
8 CUPS BEEF BOUILLION (AT ROOM TEMPERATURE)

1 #2 CAN TOMATOES (2 CUPS)
1 ONION, FINELY CHOPPED
1 STALK CELERY, FINELY CHOPPED
1/2 CLOVE GARLIC, MINCED
1 1/2 TEASPOONS SALT
1/2 TEASPOON DRIED THYME
1/2 TEASPOON DRIED BASIL
1 TEASPOON CHOPPED FRESH PARSLEY
2 TEASPOONS WORCESTERSHIRE SAUCE

1. Soak a 4-quart clay pot in water for 15 minutes.

2. Combine 2 tablespoons bulgur wheat with the ground meat, egg, soy sauce and pepper. With a light touch, form the mixture into 48 to 60 small balls. Put the meat balls in the clay pot and sprinkle them with flour.

3. Combine the beef bouillon and tomatoes with the onion, celery, garlic, salt, herbs, Worcestershire sauce and the remaining 4 tablespoons of bulgur wheat, and pour over the meat balls.

4. Cover the pot and put it in a cold oven. Set the temperature at 425 F. and bake for 1 hour. Uncover and taste for seasoning. Skim off any fat.

   Note: When removing the lid from the pot, tilt the lid so that steam escapes away from you and doesn't hit you in the face.

MUSHROOM-PEANUT BUTTER SOUP

Isabel S. Cornell

4 servings

Cooking soups in a clay cooker in the oven keeps the flavor in the soup and prevents a skin from developing on the surface. Placed on a board or mat on the table, the clay pot turns into a soup tureen.

2 MEDIUM-SIZED STALKS CELERY AND LEAVES
½ SMALL ONION
2 TABLESPOONS BUTTER
½ POUND MUSHROOMS (RESERVE 4 CAPS FOR GARNISH)
1 TEASPOON LEMON JUICE
2 TABLESPOONS FLOUR
1 TEASPOON SALT

⅛ TEASPOON WHITE PEPPER
3 CUPS CHICKEN STOCK (AT ROOM TEMPERATURE)
½ CUP DRY VERMOUTH OR WHITE WINE
3 TABLESPOONS PEANUT BUTTER
1 CUP LIGHT CREAM
2 SCALLIONS, SLICED
CHOPPED FRESH PARSLEY

1. Soak the base and cover of a 2-quart clay cooker in water for 15 minutes.

2. Chop the celery and onion very fine (or use a food processor). Sauté the celery and onion in butter in a medium frying pan for a few minutes, without browning.

3. Sprinkle the mushrooms with lemon juice and finely chop them (or use a food processor). Add the mushrooms to the celery mixture and cook a minute longer.

4. Stir in the flour, salt and pepper. Turn the mixture into the clay pot and add the chicken stock and wine.

5. Cover the pot and put it in a cold oven. Set the temperature at 425 F. and bake for 40 minutes.

6. Whisk in the peanut butter and cream. Add the sliced mushroom caps and scallions. Check the seasoning.

7. Cover and return the clay pot to the oven. Reduce the heat to 300 F. and bake 5 to 10 minutes longer. Sprinkle with chopped parsley.

Bread

FRENCH BREAD

Isabel S. Cornell

4 loaves

This recipe yields four loaves, 12 inches long by 3 or 4 inches wide. To bake them all at once, you need two 3-quart clay cookers. If you have only one, however, you can make the dough, let it rise, punch it down and refrigerate half of it to use the next day. Or you may bake single loaves in a smaller cooker.

```
1  ENVELOPE DRY YEAST
2⅓  CUPS LUKEWARM WATER
    (105 F. TO 110 F.)
6¼  CUPS FLOUR (APPROXIMATELY)
2  TABLESPOONS SALAD OIL
1½  TEASPOONS SALT
1  TEASPOON CORNSTARCH
1  TEASPOON COLD WATER
½  CUP BOILING WATER
WHITE CORNMEAL
```

1. Soak the top and bottom of one or two 3-quart clay pots in water for 15 minutes.

2. Soften the yeast in ⅓ cup of the lukewarm water. Stir in ¾ cup of the flour. Mix it well to form a ball.

3. Immerse the ball in the remaining lukewarm water. Let it stand until it rises to the surface and is light. This will take from 15 to 20 minutes.

4. In a large bowl, put 4½ cups of flour, the oil and salt. Add the yeast and water mixture and mix well.

5. Knead the dough on a lightly floured board for 8 to 10 minutes, adding up to 1 more cup of flour as needed.

6. Place the dough in a deep, oiled bowl, cover it with a damp terry towel and let it rise in a warm place until it is doubled in bulk.

7. Prepare a glaze by mixing the cornstarch with the cold water. Add it to the boiling water, stirring constantly, and cook it until it is smooth. Cool it to room temperature.

8. Punch down the dough and divide it into quarters. Roll each piece into a

rectangle, then roll it tightly into a long roll to fit the bottom of the clay pot. Pinch the ends and turn them under to seal them. Make diagonal cuts ¼-inch deep along the top of the bread. Brush the rolls with the cornstarch glaze.

9. Oil a strip of foil to fit the bottom of the clay pot and sprinkle it with cornmeal. Place the roll or rolls of dough in the pot or pots. Two narrow loaves can be baked side by side. Cover them with a damp terry towel and let them rise until doubled—about 20 to 30 minutes. Brush them again with the cornstarch glaze.

10. Put the cover on the pot or pots and place in a cold oven. Set the temperature at 450 F. and bake for 40 minutes. Uncover and bake for 5 minutes longer, if necessary, to brown the crust. When baking a single loaf in a small clay pot, check the loaf at the end of 30 minutes.

Note: The dough may be punched down after step 6 and stored, covered, in a deep, oiled bowl in the refrigerator for 24 hours. Warm the dough 10 to 15 minutes at room temperature before shaping it, as in step 8.

SAFFRON AND FENNEL BREAD

Elizabeth Colchie

1 loaf

1 CUP WARM WATER (105 F.)
⅛ TEASPOON POWDERED SAFFRON
½ TEASPOON SUGAR
1 PACKAGE ACTIVE DRY YEAST
2 TABLESPOONS OLIVE OIL
2 TEASPOONS SALT
3½ CUPS FLOUR
2 TEASPOONS FENNEL SEEDS
½ TEASPOON FRESHLY GROUND
  PEPPER

1. In a 2-cup measure or small bowl, combine the water, saffron and sugar. Stir in the yeast. Place the mixture in a warm, draft-free place to proof for 10 minutes, or until it is bubbly and increased in volume.

2. Pour the mixture into a large bowl; add the olive oil and salt and beat in the flour, a cup at a time, to make a medium-soft dough.

3. Turn the dough out on a lightly floured surface and knead it for about 10 minutes, or until it is smooth and elastic. Place it in a lightly oiled bowl, turning the dough to coat it. Cover the bowl with plastic wrap and let the dough rise in a warm place until it is at least doubled in bulk.

4. Soak the bottom of a 2-quart clay cooker in warm water for 15 minutes.

5. Punch the dough down and turn it out onto a floured surface. Roll it out to form a rough rectangle approximately 9 by 17 inches; sprinkle the fennel and

Continued from preceding page

pepper evenly over the surface. Go over the dough with a rolling pin to press in the spices.

6. Roll the dough from a short end, jelly-roll fashion, to make a tight loaf; pinch closed the bottom seam and turn under the ends and pinch them closed.

7. Wipe dry the interior of the clay cooker and place inside it a piece of parchment paper large enough to reach about 1 inch up the sides. Center the dough cylinder, seam side down, on the parchment. Cover the dish with plastic wrap and let the dough rise in a warm place about 1 hour, or until it is doubled in bulk.

8. Toward the end of the rising, soak the top of the clay pot in water for 15 minutes. When the dough is ready, dry the top, place it on the dish (plastic removed) and place it in the oven. Turn the oven to 475 F. and bake the bread for 30 minutes. Remove the cover, turn the heat to 350 F. and bake for 20 minutes longer, or until the bread is a rich golden brown.

9. Remove the pot from the oven and let the bread cool for 5 minutes. Remove the bread and let it cool completely on a rack.

SPROUTED WHEAT BREAD

Jane Moulton

1 loaf

You'll need only 2½ tablespoons of wheat for sprouting to make this recipe, but sprouted wheat is good in salads, so you'll probably want to make more. To make 2 cups of sprouts use ⅔ cup of wheat.

    Soak the wheat overnight in plenty of water. The next day, drain it and follow the directions on your sprouter, or line a colander with wet cheesecloth. Sprinkle the soaked wheat evenly over the cloth and cover it with more wet cheesecloth. Place the colander in a ceramic or stainless-steel bowl (to exclude the light) and cover it. Keep the cheesecloth damp. The wheat should be sprouted and ready for the bread on the third day. Leftovers keep in the refrigerator for several days.

1½ CUPS WARM WATER
  (105 F. TO 115 F.)
2 PACKAGES ACTIVE DRY YEAST
⅓ CUP VEGETABLE OIL OR
  MELTED BUTTER
½ CUP LIGHT OR DARK BROWN
  SUGAR
2½ CUPS WHOLE WHEAT FLOUR
  (SPOONED INTO A CUP AND
  LEVELED)
2 TEASPOONS SALT
½ CUP SPROUTED WHEAT
2½ CUPS ALL-PURPOSE FLOUR
  (APPROXIMATELY)

1. Place the water in a mixer bowl and add the yeast. Let it stand for 5 minutes. Add the oil, brown sugar and the whole wheat flour. Stir them together; add the salt and mix vigorously. Add the sprouted wheat and mix well.

2. Add enough of the all-purpose flour to make a stiff dough. The dough will leave the sides of the bowl and won't stick to a clean finger. (Without a heavy-duty mixer, the last of the flour will have to be added by hand.)

3. Turn the dough out onto a lightly floured board and knead it until it is smooth and elastic, or use the dough hook on a mixer for about 5 minutes.

4. Place the dough in a greased bowl and oil the surface of the dough. Cover and let it rise in a warm place until it is doubled in bulk—about 1 hour.

5. Soak the bottom of a 3-quart clay cooker in cold water for 15 minutes.

6. With a small piece of foil, line the bottom and 1 inch up the side of the pot.

7. Place the dough in the bottom of the pot and smooth the surface. Cover and let it rise for 25 minutes. (The dough should not be doubled in bulk.)

8. While the dough rises, soak the top of the pot in water and drain it.

9. Cover the pot and place it in a cold oven. Turn the temperature to 450 F. and bake the bread for 30 minutes.

10. Remove the cover and reduce the heat to 400 F. Bake an additional 15 to 20 minutes, or until it is done. (The bread will sound hollow when it is tapped with your fist.)

11. Turn it out of the pot and cool it on a rack.

Vegetables

BROWN RICE VEGETARIAN CASSEROLE

Joanne Will

6 servings

3 TABLESPOONS VEGETABLE OIL
1 MEDIUM-SIZED SWEET ONION, THINLY SLICED
½ TEASPOON CRUMBLED DRY MARJORAM
½ TEASPOON THYME
½ TEASPOON SAGE
1 BAY LEAF
1 CUP BROWN RICE
2 CUPS WATER
2 TABLESPOONS LIGHT SOY SAUCE

2 CUPS SLICED CELERY, DIAGONALLY SLICED
2 MEDIUM-SIZED ZUCCHINI, HALVED LENGTHWISE, DIAGONALLY SLICED
4 OUNCES FRESH MUSHROOMS, HALVED, OR QUARTERED, IF LARGE
¼ CUP SLICED UNBLEACHED ALMONDS
½ CUP CHOPPED FRESH PARSLEY (PREFERABLY ITALIAN)

1. Heat 2 tablespoons of the oil in a heavy saucepan; add the onion and cook until it is soft. Stir in the marjoram, thyme, sage and bay leaf. Cook 1 minute longer. Remove the onions and seasonings from the pan and set them aside.

2. Heat the remaining oil in the saucepan. Blend in the brown rice; stir it until it is coated with the oil. Add the water and 1 tablespoon of soy sauce and heat to boiling. Reduce the heat, cover, and simmer for 30 minutes. (The rice will finish cooking in the clay pot.)

3. Meanwhile, soak a 2-quart clay cooker in cold water for 15 minutes. Prepare the remaining vegetables.

4. Combine the rice, sautéed onion and seasonings, celery, zucchini, mushrooms and the remaining tablespoon of soy sauce in the pot. Cover it and set it in the center of a cold oven. Turn the temperature to 425 F. and bake for 30 to 40 minutes, or until the rice is cooked and the vegetables are tender.

5. Remove the pot from the oven and stir in the almonds and parsley. Serve at once.

STUFFED CABBAGE

Florence Fabricant

6 servings

1 LARGE CABBAGE (4 TO 5 POUNDS)	½ TEASPOON PAPRIKA
1 TABLESPOON COOKING OIL	1 CUP DRAINED SAUERKRAUT
1 MEDIUM-SIZED ONION, CHOPPED	1 CAN (APPROXIMATELY 1 POUND)
½ POUND LEAN GROUND BEEF	ITALIAN TOMATOES
½ POUND LEAN GROUND PORK	½ CUP RAISINS
1 LARGE CLOVE GARLIC, MINCED	3 TABLESPOONS LEMON JUICE
1 CUP COOKED RICE	3 TABLESPOONS BROWN SUGAR
1 TABLESPOON SALT	¼ CUP SWEET VERMOUTH
½ TEASPOON FRESHLY GROUND	1 BAY LEAF
BLACK PEPPER	THIN SLICES OF LEMON
½ TEASPOON DRIED THYME	1½ CUPS SOUR CREAM

1. Wash the cabbage and remove the tough outer leaves. With a sharp knife, remove the core. Parboil the cabbage, core side down, 4 to 5 minutes, to wilt the leaves. Carefully separate the leaves. Parboil any center leaves that have not wilted as you reach them. Cut the tough center spine out of each leaf.

2. Submerge a 3-quart clay cooker in cold water for 15 minutes.

3. Heat the cooking oil in a skillet and sauté the onion until it is light brown. Add the beef and pork and cook until they lose their color. Add the garlic, rice, salt, pepper, thyme and paprika.

4. Rinse the sauerkraut and squeeze it dry. Drain the clay cooker and spread the sauerkraut over the bottom.

5. Place 1 to 2 tablespoons of the meat mixture near the edge of a cabbage leaf and tightly roll the leaf around the stuffing, tucking in the sides. Place it in the pot, seam side down. Repeat with the remaining large and medium cabbage leaves. Do not attempt to stuff very small or rigid leaves.

6. Make 2 cups of finely shredded cabbage from the remaining cabbage and spread it over the stuffed cabbage rolls.

7. Combine the tomatoes, raisins, lemon juice, brown sugar and vermouth and pour the mixture over the cabbage. Place the bay leaf and lemon slices on top.

8. Cover the pot and place it in a cold oven. Turn the temperature to 450 F. and bake for 1 hour and 45 minutes. Serve directly from the clay cooker, topping each portion with a generous dollop of sour cream.

UNEXPECTED POTATOES

Michael Batterberry

6 servings

6 LARGE OVAL NEW POTATOES
  (THE SIZE OF AVERAGE BAKING
  POTATOES)
6 TABLESPOONS (¾ STICK) BUTTER
  (PREFERABLY UNSALTED)
2 TABLESPOONS RUBBED SAGE
2 TEASPOONS SALT
FRESHLY GROUND BLACK PEPPER
1 TABLESPOON FINELY MINCED
  PARSLEY

1. Soak a 4-quart clay cooker in cold water for 15 minutes.

2. Peel the potatoes (they should be as uniform in size and shape as possible) and cover them with cold water.

3. Cream together butter, sage, salt and 4–5 grinds of black pepper. This may be done by hand or food processor.

4. Line the bottom and sides of the clay cooker with a piece of buttered kitchen parchment paper.

5. From the middle of the flat side of each potato (at the point where you'd be likely to start to split a baked one) remove a "plug" with the large end of a melon ball scoop. Reserve it. With the small end of the scoop, hollow out enough space to fill with a tablespoon of the butter-sage mixture. Fill and plug with the reserved scoop of potato.

6. Arrange the potatoes, plug side up, in the clay pot. Cover and bake at 350 F. for 1½ hours. Test them for doneness with a sharp skewer. Sprinkle with parsley and salt and serve.

BAKED DEVILLED POTATOES
(POMMES DE TERRE À DIABLE)

Carol Cutler

6 servings

Usually *diable* (devil) refers to a hot sauce served with meat dishes, but that is not the case here. The name comes from the pot in which the French have traditionally baked their potatoes, a casserole which is flat on the top and bottom and has a handle, called a *diable*. The unpeeled potatoes are baked together with flavorings such as garlic, thyme, basil or bay leaves. A wet clay pot approximates the *diable*. The long, slow steaming allows the seasonings to penetrate the potatoes, and the resulting flavor is far more interesting than plain baked potatoes.

12 SMALL NEW POTATOES
3 CLOVES GARLIC, UNPEELED
2 SPRIGS THYME
1 BAY LEAF

1. Scrub the potatoes and soak them and a 2½-quart clay cooker in water for 15 minutes.

2. Drain the pot. Lift the potatoes out of the water and put them in the pot without drying them.

3. Add the seasonings to the potatoes. Cover the pot and put it in a cold oven. Turn the temperature to 400 F.

4. Turn the potatoes 2 or 3 times during the baking. It will take about 1½ hours, depending on the quality of the potatoes. Serve them hot with melted butter.

ZUCCHINI HOT POT

Isabel S. Cornell

4 servings

4 CUPS FIRMLY PACKED SHREDDED ZUCCHINI OR PART SUMMER SQUASH (PEEL BEFORE SHREDDING, IF DESIRED)
1 CARROT, SHREDDED
1 GREEN PEPPER, SHREDDED
1 ONION, SHREDDED
2 TEASPOONS INSTANT CHICKEN BOUILLON

2 TABLESPOONS FLOUR
¾ TO 1 TEASPOON SALT
½ TEASPOON POWDERED MUSTARD
⅛ TEASPOON WHITE PEPPER
½ CLOVE GARLIC, MINCED
2 TOMATOES, CUT IN THICK SLICES
3 TABLESPOONS GRATED PARMESAN CHEESE
3 TABLESPOONS MAYONNAISE

1. Soak a 2-quart clay pot in water for 15 minutes.

2. Mix the shredded vegetables in a sieve and squeeze out as much liquid as possible. In the pot, mix the vegetables with the instant bouillon, flour, salt, mustard, pepper and garlic. Arrange the tomato slices on top.

3. Cover the pot and put it in a cold oven. Set the temperature at 450 F. and bake for 40 minutes.

4. Combine the cheese and the mayonnaise and spread it on the tomato slices.

5. Return the pot to the oven, uncovered, and bake 5 minutes longer until the topping is puffed and lightly browned.

VEGETABLE AND HERB CASSEROLE (BRIAM)

Vilma Liacouras Chantiles

4 servings

Dishes like *briam* (sometimes called *briami*) are enjoyed throughout the Mediterranean area, and the French *ratatouille* is probably the most famous. The Greek version includes a handful of okra, a transplant from Africa. Serve with cheese and whole grain bread for a perfect and nutritious meal. Finish with fresh fruit, nuts, and muscatel wine.

¼ CUP VINEGAR
½ POUND FRESH OKRA OR 10-OUNCE PACKAGE FROZEN OKRA, DEFROSTED (OR SUBSTITUTE ½ POUND GREEN BEANS)
½ POUND SPANISH ONION (1 ONION)
½ POUND EGGPLANT (1 VERY SMALL)
½ POUND ZUCCHINI
1 LARGE GREEN PEPPER
½ POUND TOMATO

¼ CUP OLIVE OIL
1½ TABLESPOONS FINE CRACKED WHEAT (BULGUR), BREADCRUMBS OR WHEAT GERM
⅓ CUP FINELY MINCED PARSLEY
⅓ CUP FINELY MINCED DILL OR FRESH BASIL
1 TABLESPOON COARSE SALT
1 SMALL CLOVE GARLIC, MINCED

1. Pour the vinegar over the okra to soak for 20 minutes.

2. Soak a 2-quart clay cooker in water for 15 minutes.

3. Prepare the vegetables: cut the onion into thin slices; halve the eggplant lengthwise and cut it into slices ½-inch thick; cut the zucchini into ½-inch-thick slices; seed the green pepper and cut it into ¼-inch-thick strips; slice the tomato into slices ½-inch thick.

4. Sprinkle 1 tablespoon of oil over the bottom of the pot and sprinkle 1 tablespoon of the cracked wheat evenly over it.

5. Layer the vegetables, except for the tomatoes, so that their flavors will permeate each other. Sprinkle lightly between the layers with the oil, herbs, salt and garlic. Place the tomatoes on top and dribble over the remaining olive oil and the cracked wheat.

6. Cover the pot and place it in a cold oven. Turn the heat to 375 F. and bake for 1 hour, or until the vegetables are tender. If the liquid is too thin, drain it off into a saucepan and boil it down. You can serve the vegetables hot or cooled. The flavor is even better the next day.

TUSCAN BEANS BAKED WITH TUNA
AND LEMON (FAGIOLI STUFATI)

Giuliano Bugialli

6 servings

Though Tuscans and Florentines are often called "bean-eaters," the *cannellini,* or white kidney beans, were introduced from America relatively late in the development of Florentine cooking. Sage is often used to bring out the flavor of these beans. Tuna and lemon add the special touch in this treatment of clay-baked *cannellini.*

2 CUPS DRIED WHITE *CANNELLINI*
  BEANS
4½ CUPS COLD WATER
2 TEASPOONS SALT
10 LEAVES OF FRESH SAGE OR
  1 TO 2 TEASPOONS DRIED
1 7-OUNCE CAN OF TUNA IN OLIVE
  OIL
¼ CUP FRESH LEMON JUICE
2 TABLESPOONS OLIVE OIL
FRESHLY GROUND BLACK PEPPER

1. Soak the beans for 12 hours in the bottom of a 2- to 3-quart clay cooker in water to cover them.

2. Soak the top half of the clay cooker in water for 15 minutes.

3. Drain the beans and pour in 4½ cups of fresh water. Add the salt and the sage and cover the pot and put it in a cold oven.

4. Turn the control knob to 400 F. and bake for 1 hour. Stir the beans and bake them for another hour.

5. Break up the tuna with a fork and add it to the beans at the end of the 2 hours and bake, covered, for an additional 15 minutes.

6. Remove the casserole from the oven and gently stir in the lemon juice, olive oil and pepper. Taste for seasoning. Cover the casserole and let it stand for at least an hour before serving.

Note: This dish is even better if it is eaten cold the next day, adding a few slices of red onion to garnish it.

STUFFED PEPPERS

Paul Rubinstein

4 servings

4 LARGE GREEN PEPPERS
2 TABLESPOONS BUTTER
4 TABLESPOONS FINELY CHOPPED
  ONION
½ POUND GROUND BEEF
1 CUP COOKED RICE
2 EGGS, BEATEN
½ TEASPOON SEASONED SALT
¼ TEASPOON FRESHLY GROUND
  BLACK PEPPER
1 TEASPOON WORCESTERSHIRE
  SAUCE

1. Soak a 3-quart clay cooker in water for 15 minutes.

2. Slice the tops off the peppers and scoop out all the loose pulp and seeds. Reserve the tops.

3. In a large skillet, melt the butter, add the chopped onion, and sauté it over medium heat until it is transparent and tender.

4. Stir in the ground beef and cook until it is slightly browned.

5. Stir in the rice, eggs and seasonings and mix well until blended. Turn off the heat.

6. Stuff the peppers with the mixture and arrange them in the clay cooker.

7. Place the pepper tops on the stuffing, cover the cooker and put it in a cold oven.

8. Set the oven dial at 400 F. and bake for 1 hour and 15 minutes.

9. Serve immediately, basting the peppers with the accumulated liquid in the cooker.

Fish

RED SNAPPER NIÇOISE

Nan Mabon

4 servings

1 2½-POUND RED SNAPPER, CLEANED, GILLS REMOVED, HEAD AND TAIL LEFT ON
2 TABLESPOONS LEMON JUICE
SALT
FRESHLY GROUND PEPPER
2 TABLESPOONS OLIVE OIL
1 MEDIUM-SIZED ONION, FINELY CHOPPED
1 CLOVE GARLIC, FINELY CHOPPED

1 2-POUND CAN IMPORTED PLUM TOMATOES, DRAINED AND CHOPPED
¼-POUND OIL-CURED BLACK OLIVES, PITTED AND SLICED INTO QUARTERS
½ TEASPOON OREGANO
1 TABLESPOON CHOPPED, FRESH BASIL OR ½ TEASPOON DRY BASIL

1. Soak a 3-quart clay cooker in water for 15 minutes, then line the bottom section with foil.

2. Rub the fish all over with the lemon juice, salt and pepper and 1 tablespoon of the olive oil and put it in the pot. (If the fish is too long, remove the head and tail.)

3. Place the clay pot in the oven and set the temperature to 350 F. Bake the fish for 35 minutes.

4. While the fish is in the oven, heat the remaining tablespoon of olive oil in a large saucepan. Cook the onion and garlic over moderate heat until the onions are translucent, then add the tomatoes, olives, oregano and basil. Let them simmer for 20 minutes.

5. When the fish is done (test by flaking the flesh with a fork), pour the juices from the clay pot into the saucepan and reduce it for a few minutes over high heat. Keep the fish covered until ready to serve.

6. Lift the fish out of the pot in the foil, place it on a serving platter and remove the foil. Taste the sauce for seasoning, then pour it over the fish and serve immediately. Accompany with saffron rice.

POACHED FILLETS OF SOLE

Maurice Moore-Betty

4 servings

2 TEASPOONS BUTTER
4 FILLETS OF SOLE
¼ POUND SHRIMP, PEELED AND
  DEVEINED
1 CUP HEAVY CREAM
2 EGGS, SEPARATED
2 TEASPOONS TOMATO PASTE
2 TEASPOONS SALT
PEPPER
NUTMEG
½ CUP DRY WHITE WINE
¼ TEASPOON COARSE SALT
1 TABLESPOON CHOPPED PARSLEY

1. Soak a 2-quart clay cooker in water for 15 minutes. Drain it and brush the bottom half with the butter.

2. Cut the fish fillets in half and pull out the connecting membrane. Roll loosely and arrange each piece upright in the pot.

3. Purée the shrimp with ½ cup cream in a food processor or blender for about 25 seconds. Add the egg whites and tomato paste and turn on the motor for 25 seconds longer. Add 2 teaspoons of salt, 3 or 4 grindings from the pepper mill and a good pinch of nutmeg. Mix by turning the motor on and off once or twice.

4. Poach 1 tablespoon of the shrimp mixture in simmering water for 2 minutes. Taste it for seasoning and if more is needed, add it to the mixture in the processor bowl and mix again.

5. Spoon the mixture into the hollows of the fish fillets—a little more than a tablespoon is enough, as the mixture expands as it cooks.

6. Heat the wine to the boiling point in a small pan and pour it and the remaining ½ cup of cream into the clay pot.

7. Dust the fillets lightly with the coarse salt and cover the pot. Put the clay pot in a cold oven and turn the thermostat to 450 F. Bake for approximately half an hour.

8. Take the clay pot out of the oven and carefully lift out the fillets with a slotted spoon. Arrange them on a heated serving dish.

9. Whisk the egg yolks with a little of the liquid from the pot, and stir the mixture into the pot. There should be enough heat retained to thicken the sauce, but if not, pour it into a small clean pan and thicken it over low heat. Taste for seasoning and pour it over the fish fillets

10. Sprinkle with finely chopped parsley and serve with steamed potatoes.

AROMATIC LOBSTER

Paul Rubinstein

2 servings

1 2- TO 3-POUND LIVE MAINE LOBSTER OR 2 1- TO 1½-POUND LIVE MAINE LOBSTERS
1 CUP BOTTLED CLAM JUICE
½ CUP DRY WHITE WINE
1 TABLESPOON LEMON JUICE
½ CUP FINELY MINCED SHALLOTS
1 TEASPOON DRIED TARRAGON
2 TEASPOONS DRIED PARSLEY

1 LARGE STALK FRESH DILL (OR 1 TABLESPOON DRIED DILL WEED)
¼ TEASPOON FRESHLY GROUND BLACK PEPPER
4 TABLESPOONS (½ STICK) BUTTER
4 TABLESPOONS ALL-PURPOSE FLOUR
ADDITIONAL CLAM JUICE IF NEEDED

1. Soak a 3-quart clay cooker in water for 15 minutes.

2. In a large pot, bring enough water to immerse the lobsters to a boil. Plunge the lobsters into the rapidly boiling water and boil for 2 minutes. Remove them immediately with tongs.

3. Place the clam juice, wine, lemon juice, shallots, tarragon, parsley, dill and pepper in the clay cooker, add the lobsters, cover, and place in a cold oven. Turn the oven indicator to 425 F. and bake for 20 minutes if you are using 2 small lobsters, 30 minutes if 1 larger one.

4. When they are done, remove the lobsters from the pot; split them in half using a sharp chef's knife or cleaver, and remove the sac at the back of the head. Twist off the large claws, crack them and remove the meat, all in one piece if possible, from each claw. Remove the coral and tomalley from the body cavity of each lobster and replace it with the claw meat. Wrap the lobster in a damp towel to keep it warm while preparing the sauce.

5. Strain the liquid left in the pot and discard the dill stalk. In a bowl, mash the tomalley and coral with a fork to make a smooth texture.

6. Melt the butter in a saucepan, add the flour and stir it well to make a smooth paste. Add the tomalley and coral and cook for 2 minutes over medium heat. Add the strained liquid, a little at a time, until it is all absorbed, stirring constantly. If the sauce is very thick, add extra clam juice to bring it to a medium-thick consistency.

7. Serve the lobsters, spooning some sauce over the claw meat and tail, and bring the rest of the sauce to the table in a sauceboat.

BAKED BASS WITH EGG SAUCE

Paul Rubinstein

4 to 6 servings

1 5- TO 6-POUND STRIPED BASS, CLEANED, WITH HEAD AND TAIL REMOVED
1 CUP CHOPPED ONIONS
8 STRIPS HICKORY-SMOKED BACON
2 STALKS CELERY, CUT INTO 1-INCH PIECES
1 TURNIP, PEELED AND CUT INTO QUARTERS
2 TABLESPOONS WHITE VINEGAR
1 CUP CLAM JUICE
½ TEASPOON FRESHLY GROUND BLACK PEPPER
1 POUND (4 STICKS) BUTTER
6 HARD-COOKED EGGS
½ TEASPOON SEASONED SALT

1. Soak a 3-quart clay cooker in water for 15 minutes.

2. Wash the bass under cold running water and pat it dry with paper towels. Stuff the cavity with chopped onions, then wrap the fish with the bacon strips, securing each with a toothpick.

3. Place the bacon-wrapped fish in the bottom of the clay cooker; add the celery, turnip, vinegar, clam juice and pepper. Cover the pot and place it in a cold oven; turn the oven control to 400 F. and bake for 1 hour and 20 minutes.

4. During the last 15 minutes of baking time, melt the butter in the top of a double boiler over simmering water (you will have 2 cups). Peel and chop the hard-cooked eggs; add them to the butter. Stir in the seasoned salt, and keep the egg sauce hot until serving time.

5. To serve the bass, remove it carefully from the cooker using two spatulas or two large spoons. Remove the bacon strips and pull out and discard the onions from the cavity (as much as possible without breaking up the meat). Serve on a warm platter with the egg sauce in a sauceboat.

Poultry

BAKED CHICKEN STUFFED WITH WILD THYME
(POULET AU SERPOLET)

Raymond Sokolov

4 servings

1 CHICKEN, 3 TO 3½ POUNDS
SALT
PEPPER
1 GENEROUS HANDFUL (ABOUT
  ½ PACKAGE) IMPORTED FRENCH
  WILD THYME *(SERPOLET),* OR
  SUBSTITUTE FRESH THYME
  IN BRANCHES
8 TABLESPOONS (1 STICK) BUTTER
1 CUP DRY WHITE WINE
¼ CUP HEAVY CREAM

1. Soak a 2- to 3-quart clay cooker (one just large enough to hold the chicken) in enough water to cover it for ½ hour.

2. Preheat the oven to 450 F.

3. Rub the chicken inside and out with salt and pepper.

4. Insert the wild thyme and the stick of butter into the chicken's cavity. Sew up or truss the opening and legs.

5. Drain the casserole and put the chicken in it. Pour the white wine over it, cover and put the chicken in the oven.

6. Cook the chicken for about 1 hour, or until the juices from the thickest part of the thigh run clear when the thigh is pierced with a trussing needle. If you insist on a deeply browned chicken, you should peek at your bird after 45 minutes and finish it, uncovered, if you aren't satisfied with its color up to that point.

7. When the chicken is done, remove it to a serving platter and keep it warm.

8. Remove as much fat as you can from the cooking liquid and strain it into a saucepan. Over low heat, whisk in the heavy cream. Serve it hot, as a sauce with the chicken.

TURKEY TERRINE

Elizabeth Colchie

1 large loaf

3 POUNDS FRESH TURKEY THIGH

Marinade:
4 JUNIPER BERRIES
1 CRUMBLED BAY LEAF
¼ TEASPOON COARSE SALT
¼ TEASPOON PEPPERCORNS
¼ TEASPOON THYME
3 TABLESPOONS DRY VERMOUTH

Forcemeat:
1 POUND BONELESS STEWING VEAL
½ POUND FRESH PORK FAT,
   IN PIECES
1 SMALL CLOVE GARLIC
1 BAY LEAF
½ TEASPOON JUNIPER BERRIES

¼ TEASPOON WHOLE ALLSPICE
2 TEASPOONS COARSE SALT
½ TEASPOON THYME
¼ TEASPOON GROUND PEPPER
1 CUP CRUMBLED STALE WHITE
   BREAD
½ CUP BOILING WATER
2 EGGS

Other Ingredients:
½ POUND FRESH PORK FAT, IN THIN
   SHEETS
¼ POUND WESTPHALIAN HAM
   (OR *PROSCIUTTO*), CUT IN
   2 THICK SLICES

1. Skin and bone the turkey, saving the bones for another use. There should be about 1½ pounds of meat. Cut ½ pound of meat into ½-inch dice.

2. In a mortar, grind the juniper, bay leaf, salt, pepper and thyme. Add the vermouth and mix well; combine this mixture with the diced turkey in a small bowl.

3. Chop the remaining turkey fairly fine in a food processor, if possible, or grind it. Turn it into a large bowl and add the veal to the processor and chop it fairly fine; add it to the bowl. Chop the pork fat quite coarsely; add it to the bowl.

4. Put a 2-quart clay cooker in water to soak for 15 minutes.

5. Crush the garlic to a purée. In a mortar, crush the bay leaf, juniper, allspice, salt, thyme and pepper. Combine in a small bowl with the garlic, bread and boiling water and beat to form a paste; add the eggs and beat well. Add to the meat mixture and beat vigorously to mix well. Add the diced turkey and mix.

6. Line the bottom half of the clay cooker with half the pork sheets; spoon in about one-third of the forcemeat and flatten it. Cut 1 slice Westphalian into ¼-inch strips and arrange them lengthwise on the forcemeat. Spoon on another third of the forcemeat and press down. Cut up and arrange the other piece of ham on it; spoon on the remaining forcemeat and press down. Cover with the remaining pork fat. Cover the pot.

7. Place the pot in the oven and turn the heat to 375 F. and bake for 1 hour and 45 minutes, or until the juices run clear and the terrine registers 170 F. to 180 F. Uncover and place a pan or dish on top of the terrine to fit as closely as possible and place weights in it. Let the terrine cool for several hours; refrigerate 1 to 3 days before serving. If you wish to keep the terrine longer, pour on a layer of melted lard to cover it completely.

CHINESE CHICKEN BAKED IN A CLAY ROBE

Michael Tong

4 servings

This recipe takes some advance planning, but the surprise is worth the effort. You will need ordinary potter's clay, which can be bought in 15-pound bags from potters' shops or craft stores, as well as lotus leaves, which are optional.

2 POUNDS CLAY, WETTED
10 LOTUS LEAVES* OR OTHER
    FRESH LEAVES
1 2-POUND FRYING CHICKEN,
    WASHED AND PATTED DRY

Marinade:
1 TEASPOON SALT
2 TABLESPOONS DARK SOY SAUCE
1 TEASPOON SESAME OIL*
2 TABLESPOONS DRY SHERRY
1 TEASPOON SUGAR

Stuffing:
2 TABLESPOONS THINLY SLICED
    VIRGINIA HAM
2 TABLESPOONS THINLY SLICED
    WATER CHESTNUTS
1 TABLESPOON SOAKED, THINLY
    SLICED ORIENTAL MUSHROOMS*
2 TABLESPOONS FINELY CHOPPED
    SCALLIONS
1 TABLESPOON FINELY CHOPPED
    FRESH GINGER
½ TEASPOON MINCED GARLIC

1. Brush the chicken inside and out with the marinade and let it stand for 2 hours.

2. Combine the stuffing ingredients and mix them well. Stuff the chicken cavity, but do not sew it up.

3. Place the leaves on a tray so they overlap. Center the chicken on the leaves, breast-side up. Draw the leaves up over the chicken so that it is completely wrapped; over-wrap in two thicknesses of aluminum foil.

4. Flatten a handful of wet clay, and begin to slap it on the wrapped chicken. Continue until the chicken is completely encased in clay. Be sure to mark the outside to identify the breast.

5. Preheat the oven to 350 F.

6. Place the chicken on a shallow baking dish, and bake for 1½ hours. Raise the heat to 400 F., and continue baking for another 1½ hours.

7. To serve, place the clay-wrapped chicken on a large wooden tray, breast-side up. Cover it with a large dinner napkin or towel and bring it to the table. Remove the napkin and display the chicken to your guests. Recover it with the napkin and give it a judicious rap with a wooden mallet to break apart the clay shell. Fold back the foil, then the leaves. Pass the chicken so that the guests can help themselves—the chicken will be fork tender.

*These ingredients are available in Oriental grocery stores.

CURRY OF CHICKEN AND EGGPLANT

Florence Fabricant

6 to 8 servings

1 POUND EGGPLANT
5 TEASPOONS SALT
2 TABLESPOONS BUTTER
16 CHICKEN DRUMSTICKS OR
  8 DRUMSTICKS AND 8 THIGHS
1½ CUPS SLICED ONION
FRESHLY GROUND BLACK PEPPER
1 TEASPOON GROUND CUMIN

1 TEASPOON GROUND CORIANDER
½ TEASPOON GROUND GINGER
¼ TEASPOON CAYENNE PEPPER
½ POUND MUSHROOMS, SLICED
JUICE OF 1 LEMON
2 TEASPOONS CORNSTARCH
½ CUP PLAIN YOGURT

1. Cut the eggplant into 1-inch squares, dust it with 3 teaspoons of the salt and set aside for 30 minutes.

2. Submerge both halves of a 3-quart clay cooker in cold water for 15 minutes.

3. While the clay pot is soaking, heat the butter in a large skillet. Lightly brown the chicken pieces and remove them to a platter. Turn off the heat under the skillet.

4. Drain the clay cooker and scatter the onions in the bottom. Season the chicken pieces with 1 teaspoon salt and place them over the onions. Dust them with freshly ground pepper.

5. Rinse and dry the eggplant. Place the skillet, with the butter remaining from the chicken, over medium-high heat and sauté the eggplant, stirring it for 3 minutes. Sprinkle it with cumin, coriander, ginger and cayenne and continue to stir in the skillet for 3 minutes longer. Stir in the mushrooms. Then spoon the mushroom-eggplant mixture over the chicken.

6. Sprinkle lemon juice over the mixture, cover it, and place it in a cold oven. Turn the oven temperature to 450 F. and bake for 1 hour.

7. Dissolve the cornstarch in the yogurt.

8. Transfer the chicken and vegetables to a serving platter or the top half of the clay cooker. Pour the cooking liquid into a saucepan, stir in the yogurt mixture and simmer for a minute or two, until the sauce has thickened. Season it with salt and pepper if necessary. Pour the sauce over the chicken and vegetables on the serving platter or, if you wish to present the dish in the clay cooker, return the chicken and vegetables to the bottom half. Pour on the sauce and serve.

DUCK WITH LENTILS

Carole Lalli

4 servings

1 POUND LENTILS
1 LARGE DUCK (5 TO 7 POUNDS)
SALT
FRESHLY GROUND PEPPER
4 TABLESPOONS RESERVED
    DUCK FAT
1 STALK CELERY, FINELY CHOPPED
1 CARROT, FINELY CHOPPED
1 ONION, FINELY CHOPPED

AN HERB BOUQUET CONSISTING OF
    4 SPRIGS PARSLEY, ½ BAY LEAF,
    2 CLOVES GARLIC, ¼ TEASPOON
    THYME, ALL TIED TOGETHER
    IN CHEESECLOTH
1 TO 1½ CUPS CHICKEN OR DUCK
    STOCK AND WATER RESERVED
    FROM LENTILS

1. Blanch the lentils in boiling salted water to cover for 10 minutes and drain, reserving the liquid.

2. Quarter the duck, salt and pepper it, and broil it on a rack in a broiling pan for 10 minutes on each side. Reserve 4 tablespoons of the duck fat which will have accumulated in the pan.

3. Soak a 3-quart clay cooker in cold water for 15 minutes.

4. In the reserved duck fat, soften the celery, carrot and onion for 10 minutes. Add the lentils, salt and pepper and stir to mix the vegetables and to moisten the lentils with the fat.

5. Put the lentil mixture in the clay cooker. Add the duck pieces and the herb bouquet. Pour over a combination of the reserved lentil water and chicken stock so that liquid reaches nearly to the top of the lentils.

6. Cover and place the pot in a cold oven. Turn the thermostat to 400 F. and bake for 1 hour.

7. Serve with a watercress, orange and endive salad.

Note: If there are any leftovers, chop the skinned and boned duck meat, add it to the lentils, toss them with a vinaigrette, garnish with chopped red onions and parsley and serve the salad cold.

DUCK IN MADEIRA

Nathalie Dupree

2 to 3 servings

1 5½-POUND DUCK
4 TABLESPOONS (½ STICK) BUTTER
1 SLICED ONION
1 SLICED CARROT
HERB BOUQUET CONSISTING OF 3
    SPRIGS PARSLEY, ½ BAY LEAF,
    SPRIG OR PINCH OF THYME
½ CUP MADEIRA
1 CUP GIBLET STOCK OR CANNED
    BEEF BOUILLON
2 TEASPOONS CORNSTARCH

1. Soak a 3-quart clay cooker in water for 15 minutes.

2. Clean and truss the duck. Prick all along the back and base of the breast and thighs.

3. In a frying pan, brown the duck slowly in 2 tablespoons of the butter.

4. Spread the vegetables in the bottom of the pot and place the duck on them. Add the herb bouquet and the Madeira.

5. Cover the pot and place it in a cold oven. Turn the heat to 450 F. and cook for 1 hour. Remove the cover and continue cooking 5 to 10 minutes longer to crisp the duck.

6. Strain the juices from the pot and skim off the fat. You may serve the juices as they are, or they can be enriched and thickened. Dissolve the cornstarch in the cup of stock and add it to the juices in a saucepan. Bring the liquid to a boil, stirring until it is thickened. Add the remaining butter if you prefer a richer sauce.

CORNISH HEN WITH CARROTS AND POTATOES

Elizabeth Colchie

2 servings

Although this recipe is so simple that it appears to be self-evident, the taste of the dish will justify its explanation. The special qualities of the clay cooker are admirably demonstrated by this basic recipe: the hen (or any other bird) roasts evenly without drying out; the vegetables steam without added liquid, absorbing the meat and herb flavors; the tastes blend in a way that cannot be accomplished in other cooking devices. Use this simple recipe, then, as a formula for further experimentation with other poultry, root vegetables and herbs, for it is well-suited to the clay cooker.

4 TO 5 MEDIUM-SIZED CARROTS,
   PEELED AND TRIMMED
2 MINCED SHALLOTS
1 GOOD-SIZED CORNISH HEN, ABOUT
   1½ POUNDS (FRESH, NOT FROZEN,
   IF POSSIBLE)
6 MEDIUM-SIZED NEW POTATOES,
   SCRUBBED
1 TEASPOON THYME
SALT
PEPPER

1. Soak a 2-quart clay cooker in water for 15 minutes.

2. Place the carrots in the bottom, scatter the shallots over them and place the hen on top. Arrange the potatoes around the bird and sprinkle with thyme, salt and pepper. Cover with the soaked top, place the pot in the oven and turn the heat to 425 F. Bake for 1 hour and 15 minutes, or until the hen is lightly browned.

3. Carve the hen and arrange it on a heated serving dish along with the vegetables. Pour on the juices, or serve, as a sauce, separately in a warmed sauceboat.

CHICKEN IN RED WINE

Ruth Ellen Church

6 servings

1 ROASTING CHICKEN OR CAPON,
   5 TO 7 POUNDS
2 CUPS DRY RED WINE, SUCH AS
   BEAUJOLAIS OR ZINFANDEL
SALT
FRESHLY GROUND PEPPER
GIBLETS AND LIVER FROM THE
   CHICKEN
3 CUPS COOKED RICE

2 MEDIUM-SIZED ONIONS, CHOPPED
8 TABLESPOONS (1 STICK) BUTTER
¼ CUP MINCED PARSLEY
1 CUP CHOPPED PISTACHIO NUTS
1 CUP SEEDLESS RAISINS OR
   CURRANTS
¼ TEASPOON CINNAMON
¼ TEASPOON GROUND CORIANDER

1. Soak a 6-quart clay pot in cold water while you make the stuffing and fill the bird.

2. Wipe the chicken, inside and out, with wet paper towels. Sprinkle the inside with a little of the wine and salt and pepper it lightly.

3. Simmer the giblets in water until they are tender, removing the liver as soon as it is done. Reserve the giblet broth. Chop the giblets and add them to the rice.

4. Sauté the onions in 7 tablespoons of butter and add them to the rice, with parsley, pistachio nuts, raisins or currants and the seasonings. Fill the chicken cavity and sew the openings.

5. Rub the bird with the remaining butter and place it in the pot. Pour the wine over it and cover the pot. Place it in a cold oven and turn the heat to 450 F.

Continued from preceding page

Roast the chicken for 2 hours (longer for a larger bird), uncovering and basting it for the last 15 minutes to brown.

6. Test for doneness by moving the drumstick, which should move freely.

7. If you wish, you may pour the liquid into a saucepan, simmer it with the giblet water and thicken it with arrowroot.

ROAST QUAIL WITH RAISINS
(QUAGLIE ARROSTI)

Nicola Zanghi

4 servings

1 CUP MARSALA WINE
1½ CUPS RAISINS
SALT
FRESHLY GROUND PEPPER
8 5- TO 6-OUNCE QUAILS, AT ROOM
   TEMPERATURE
2 TEASPOONS MARJORAM OR SAGE
8 THIN SLICES *PROSCIUTTO*
½ CUP THINLY SLICED ONIONS
16 SMALL PEELED NEW POTATOES
½ CUP CHICKEN STOCK

1. Warm the Marsala and pour it over the raisins. Put them aside to soak for an hour.

2. Soak a 3-quart clay cooker in water for 15 minutes.

3. Salt and pepper the quails, inside and out. Sprinkle a little marjoram or sage into each cavity. Wrap a slice of *prosciutto* around each bird, fastening it with a toothpick.

4. Spread the onions on the bottom of the pot. Arrange the birds and potatoes on top of them. Add the Marsala and raisins, the stock and the remaining herb.

5. Cover the pot and put it in a cold oven. Turn the gauge to 400 F. and bake for 30 minutes. Lower the temperature to 350 F. and bake for a further 20 to 30 minutes.

6. Remove the quails and potatoes to a heated serving platter and keep them warm while you prepare the sauce.

7. Pour the juices into a saucepan and reduce the liquid over high heat until it is the consistency of heavy cream. Spoon a little of the sauce over the quail and serve the rest in a warm sauceboat.

SLIGHTLY CHINESE CHICKEN

Jane Moulton

4 servings

1 POUND FRESH MUSHROOMS,
  SLICED
1 CUP BROWN RICE
CUT-UP GIBLETS (OPTIONAL)
1 MEDIUM-SIZED ONION, PEELED
  AND CHOPPED
1 CLOVE GARLIC, MINCED FINE
½ TEASPOON SZECHUAN PEPPER*
  (OPTIONAL)

3 CUPS CHICKEN BROTH
1 SMALL ORANGE
1 MEDIUM-SIZED ONION, PEELED
½ TEASPOON FIVE-SPICE
  SEASONING*
1 WHOLE BROILER-FRYER, ABOUT
  2½ TO 3 POUNDS
2 TEASPOONS SESAME OIL*
¼ TEASPOON SALT

1. Soak a 3-quart clay cooker according to directions. If the base is unglazed, line it with parchment paper; if glazed, grease it with oil.

2. Into the bottom half of the clay cooker, put the mushrooms, uncooked brown rice, giblets (if used), onion, garlic, and ¼ teaspoon of Szechuan pepper. Mix them well. Pour the broth over the mixture and mix well again.

3. Remove the skin from each end of the orange; slice it into 4 crosswise slices, removing any seeds. (Keep the peel on.) Slice the onion into 4 crosswise slices. Sprinkle each orange and onion slice with ⅛ teaspoon of five-spice seasoning. Sprinkle another ⅛ teaspoon of the powder into the cavity of the chicken.

4. Place alternate pieces of orange and onion in the chicken cavity. If they don't all fit, place the remainder on top of the rice mixture. Twist the wings behind the back of the chicken, and place it on top of the rice in the casserole. Spread sesame oil over the exposed surface of the chicken; sprinkle with the remaining ¼ teaspoon of the five-spice seasoning and the salt, and rub in well.

5. Cover with the soaked lid and place the cooker in a cold oven. Turn the thermostat to 450 F. and bake for 1 hour and 45 minutes.

6. Place the chicken on a platter and remove the onion and orange slices. Fluff the rice mixture and serve directly from the casserole. Cut the chicken in quarters and serve it hot with the rice and slices of orange and onion.

*These ingredients are available in Oriental grocery stores.

ROAST DUCK WITH APPLE STUFFING

Paul Rubinstein

2 servings

½ CUP WATER
8 TABLESPOONS (1 STICK) BUTTER
1 MEDIUM-SIZED ONION, CHOPPED
½ LOAF STALE WHITE BREAD,
  CRUSTS TRIMMED, CUT INTO
  ½-INCH CUBES
4 APPLES, PEELED, CORED AND CUT
  INTO ½-INCH CHUNKS

1 TEASPOON GROUND THYME
1 TEASPOON SALT
½ TEASPOON FRESHLY GROUND
  BLACK PEPPER
1 TABLESPOON VEGETABLE
  SHORTENING
1 4- TO 5-POUND DUCKLING,
  OVEN READY

1. Soak a 3-quart clay cooker in water for 15 minutes.

2. Bring the water to a boil in a medium-sized saucepan, add the butter and chopped onions and simmer until the butter melts and the onion softens and becomes transparent.

3. Add the bread crumbs and the apple chunks, season with thyme, ½ teaspoon salt and the pepper and toss until well blended. Turn off the heat.

4. Heat a large cast-iron skillet over high heat and melt the vegetable shortening in it. Handling the duck with a long pair of tongs, brown the skin of the duck on all sides in the skillet, being careful not to break the skin.

5. When browned, allow the duck to cool sufficiently to handle it. Then stuff the cavity with the prepared stuffing mixture, truss the duck, place it in the clay cooker breast-side down, and sprinkle it with the remaining salt.

6. Cover the cooker and place it in a cold oven; set the oven dial at 425 F. and set the timer for 1 hour.

7. After the first hour, uncover the cooker and turn the duck breast-side up. Recover and bake for another 40 minutes.

8. To serve, remove the duck and keep it warm on a platter. Pour the liquid from the cooker into a saucepan. Bring it to a simmer, skim off as much fat as possible, and use the remaining liquid as a gravy. If there is not enough liquid, add a little red wine or Madeira.

Meats

MEXICAN PORK WITH ORANGE JUICE

Diana Kennedy

4 servings

3½ POUNDS RIB END PORK LOIN (IT
   SHOULD HAVE SOME FAT ON IT)
3 CLOVES GARLIC, PEELED
2 TEASPOONS COARSE SALT
1½ TEASPOONS LEAF OREGANO
10 PEPPERCORNS
2 SMALL ORANGES

1. Pierce the meat all over with the point of a sharp knife.

2. Crush the garlic together with the salt, oregano and peppercorns and moisten with the juice of half an orange.

3. Rub this seasoning well into the meat and set it aside for a minimum of 2 hours.

4. Soak a 3-quart clay pot in water for 15 minutes.

5. Place the pork in the clay cooker. Moisten it with the juice of the other orange half. Add the squeezed orange halves to the pot. Cover and place it on the top shelf of an unheated oven. Set the oven temperature at 375 F. and bake for 1 hour.

6. At the end of the hour, the top of the meat should be slightly browned and there should be about ½ cup liquid at the bottom of the cooker (if there is more, drain off a little). Turn the meat, baste it with the juices, cover the pot, and return it to the oven for an hour longer.

7. Turn the oven temperature up to 400 F. Remove the pot and drain the juices into a saucepan. Turn the meat again. Put the uncovered pot back in the oven and bake for 20 minutes to brown the top of the pork. Turn the meat once again to brown it on the other side, and bake for another 20 minutes.

8. Meanwhile, skim the pan juices of most of the fat. Add the juice of the second orange and reduce the sauce quickly over high heat to concentrate the flavor. Pass it separately in a sauceboat or spoon it over the sliced meat at the moment of serving.

ARGENTINE BRAISED BEEF (BEEF GUISADO)

Ruth Ellen Church

4 to 6 servings

2 POUNDS BEEF ROUND CUT 1½
  INCHES THICK
1 CLOVE GARLIC
1 TEASPOON SALT
¼ TEASPOON BLACK PEPPER
2 TABLESPOONS LIME OR LEMON
  JUICE
1½ CUPS CHOPPED ONIONS
1 CUP SLICED CARROTS
¼ TEASPOON MARJORAM
1 CAN (8 OUNCES) TOMATO SAUCE
½ CUP BEEF STOCK, CONSOMMÉ
  OR BOUILLON

1. Soak a 4- to 6-quart clay cooker in cold water for 15 minutes.

2. Rub the beef with the cut clove of garlic, or if you prefer, chop the garlic and include it with the other ingredients.

3. Sprinkle the meat with salt, pepper and lime or lemon juice. Place it in the clay pot and scatter the onions and carrots over the meat. Sprinkle with marjoram. Combine the tomato sauce and beef stock and pour them into the pot.

4. Put the pot in a cold oven and turn the heat to 425 F. Bake for 1½ hours.

BEEF BURGUNDY

Emanuel and Madeline Greenberg

6 servings

3 POUNDS LEAN BONELESS CHUCK,
  CUBED
6 CARROTS, SCRAPED AND CUT IN
  LARGE PIECES
12 SMALL WHITE ONIONS, PEELED
12 LARGE MUSHROOMS
4 TOMATOES, HALVED AND SEEDED
3 SHALLOTS, MINCED (OR WHITE
  PART OF 6 SCALLIONS)
1 CLOVE GARLIC, MINCED
1 TEASPOON DRIED MARJORAM
SALT TO TASTE
PEPPER TO TASTE
2 CUPS DRY RED WINE

1. Soak a 3-quart clay cooker in water for 15 minutes.

2. Place the beef cubes in the pot. Add the carrots, white onions, mushrooms, and tomatoes. Sprinkle with shallots, garlic, marjoram, salt and pepper. Pour the wine over the meat and vegetables.

3. Cover the pot and place it in the center of a cold oven. Set the oven at 400 F. Cook for about 2 hours, or until the meat is tender.

4. Pour the liquid from the cooker into a small saucepan and boil it down to reduce it by half. Correct the seasoning and thicken it, if desired.

5. Spoon some of the sauce over the meat and vegetables and serve the rest in a sauceboat.

BEEF RAGOUT WITH OLIVES

Paula J. Buchholz

8 servings

¼ CUP OLIVE OIL
2 TABLESPOONS BUTTER
3 POUNDS BONELESS BEEF STEW
  MEAT, CUT IN 1½-INCH CUBES
1 CUP THINLY SLICED LEEKS
1 CLOVE GARLIC, MINCED
1½ CUPS THINLY SLICED CARROTS
1½ CUPS DRY WHITE WINE
1 CAN (16 OUNCES) TOMATOES,
  BROKEN UP

¼ CUP CHOPPED FRESH PARSLEY
SALT TO TASTE
FRESHLY GROUND BLACK PEPPER
  TO TASTE
3 ZUCCHINI, CUT IN 1-INCH-THICK
  SLICES
1 CAN (8½ OUNCES) QUARTERED
  ARTICHOKES, DRAINED
½ CUP SLICED RIPE OLIVES

1. Soak a 2-quart clay cooker in water for 15 minutes.

2. Heat the olive oil and butter in a large skillet. Brown the beef cubes on all sides and transfer them to the clay cooker.

3. Lightly sauté the leeks and garlic, then stir them into the beef along with the carrots, wine, tomatoes, parsley, salt and pepper.

4. Cover and bake in a 475 F. oven for 1½ hours, until the meat is tender.

5. Add the zucchini, artichokes and olives and cook about 10 minutes longer.

BRISKET WITH APPLES AND CARAWAY

Elizabeth Colchie

4 to 5 servings

3 CUPS SLICED, TART APPLES
  (CORED, BUT NOT PEELED)
3 CUPS SLICED ONIONS
1 SLICE BREAD, PREFERABLY RYE,
  CUT UP
2 TEASPOONS CARAWAY SEEDS
3 POUNDS BEEF BRISKET, VERY
  WELL TRIMMED OF FAT AND
  DUSTED WITH FLOUR
½ TEASPOON SALT
¼ TEASPOON BLACK PEPPER
1 TABLESPOON RED WINE VINEGAR

1. Soak a 2-quart clay cooker in water for 15 minutes.

2. Line the bottom of the pot with parchment paper.

3. In the pot, arrange half the apples, half the onions, the bread and 1 teaspoon of the caraway. Place the meat on top, sprinkle it with salt and pepper, and spread the remaining apples, onions and caraway seeds on top.

4. Place the pot in the oven, turn the heat to 450 F. and bake the meat for 2½ hours, or until it is very tender.

5. Remove the brisket from the pot and skim off any fat. Pour the apple-onion mixture into a food mill and purée it into a saucepan. Add the vinegar, and additional salt and pepper to taste. Thin the purée, if necessary, with water.

6. Slice the meat and arrange it on a heated platter. Heat the sauce through and pour it over the meat.

TAGINE OF LAMB WITH PRUNES

Paula J. Buchholz

8 servings

3 TABLESPOONS BUTTER
3 TABLESPOONS OLIVE OIL
1 LARGE ONION, THINLY SLICED
1 CLOVE GARLIC, MINCED
2 TEASPOONS SALT
1 TEASPOON GROUND GINGER
1 TEASPOON GROUND CINNAMON
½ TEASPOON FRESHLY GROUND
  PEPPER
¼ TEASPOON POWDERED SAFFRON

3 POUNDS BONELESS LAMB, CUT
  IN 1½-INCH CUBES
1 PACKAGE (12 OUNCES) PITTED
  PRUNES SOAKED IN 2 CUPS OF
  WATER FOR 1 HOUR
2 TABLESPOONS HONEY
2 TABLESPOONS LEMON JUICE
2 TABLESPOONS TOASTED SESAME
  SEEDS

1. Soak a 2-quart clay cooker in water for 15 minutes.

2. Heat the butter and oil in a large skillet. Add the onions, garlic, salt, ginger, cinnamon, pepper and saffron. Sauté them for about 5 minutes.

3. Place the lamb cubes in the clay cooker. Add the onion mixture and stir to mix well. Cover and place it in a 475 F. oven for 1 hour and 15 minutes.

4. Fold in the drained prunes and cook 15 minutes longer.

5. Stir in the honey and lemon juice and garnish with the sesame seeds.

BRAISED VEAL CHOPS WITH MUSHROOMS

Carole Lalli

4 servings

3 SCALLIONS	1½ TABLESPOONS BUTTER
1 LARGE CARROT	(PREFERABLY UNSALTED)
1 CELERY STALK	1 POUND SMALL MUSHROOMS, CUT
4 ¾-INCH-THICK VEAL CHOPS	INTO THICK SLICES
(LOIN, RIB, OR SHOULDER)	½ TEASPOON LEMON JUICE
¾ TEASPOON SALT	1 CUP DRY WHITE WINE
PEPPER	1 TEASPOON DRIED ROSEMARY
1½ TABLESPOONS OLIVE OIL	3 THIN SLICES *PROSCIUTTO*

1. Soak a 2-quart clay cooker in water for at least 15 minutes.

2. Mince together the scallions, carrot and celery.

3. Trim any excess fat from the chops; sprinkle them with about ¼ teaspoon of salt and pepper to taste.

4. Heat the oil and butter and brown the chops on both sides; remove them to a plate. Add the minced vegetables and stir over medium heat for 4 to 5 minutes; add them to the plate.

5. Sauté the mushrooms in the skillet over fairly high heat, adding oil if necessary; toss the mushrooms with the remaining ½ teaspoon of salt and pepper to taste and the lemon juice. Spoon them into a dish and reserve.

6. Add the wine to the skillet and boil over high heat, stirring and scraping, until the liquid is reduced to ½ cup. Set it aside.

7. Spread half the minced vegetable mixture in the bottom of the clay cooker. Sprinkle with ½ teaspoon rosemary. Arrange the chops on top and cover them with the mushrooms. Sliver the ham, sprinkle it over the mushrooms and top with the remaining vegetables and rosemary. Pour in the wine.

8. Place the clay cooker in the center of a cold oven and turn the heat to 425 F. Bake for about 40 minutes, or until the meat is tender. Arrange the chops and vegetables on a platter. Pour on some sauce and pass the remainder in a sauceboat. *Risotto* is a good accompaniment.

SADDLE OF VENISON WITH
MUSHROOM-SOUR CREAM SAUCE

Lyn Stallworth

6 servings

1 3-POUND SADDLE OF VENISON,
   FRESH OR FROZEN
1 QUART BUTTERMILK
2 OUNCES GIN
6 JUNIPER BERRIES
2 BAY LEAVES
¼ CUP DRIED IMPORTED
   MUSHROOMS
½ CUP BOILING WATER

8 BACON STRIPS
2 MEDIUM-SIZED ONIONS, SLICED
DRY VERMOUTH
1 TABLESPOON FLOUR MIXED WITH
   2 TABLESPOONS WATER
RED CURRANT JELLY
¼ CUP SOUR CREAM
SALT
PEPPER

1. If the venison is frozen, don't bother to defrost it. Place it in a deep bowl that holds it comfortably, and pour the buttermilk over it to cover. Add the gin, juniper berries and bay leaves. Cover the bowl with plastic wrap and let the venison marinate for 2 to 4 days in the refrigerator.

2. Before you prepare the venison, soak the mushrooms in the boiling water until they become soft and the soaking water turns the color of strong tea. Drain the mushrooms and reserve the water. Cut off and discard any bits of hard stem and chop the mushrooms and reserve them.

3. Soak a 3-quart clay cooker in water for 15 minutes.

4. Line the soaked clay pot with 4 strips of bacon and half the onion slices. Wash off the venison and discard the marinade. Pat the venison dry and place it in the pot. Cover it with the rest of the onion slices and top it with the remaining strips of bacon. Pour on the mushroom soaking liquid and cover the pot.

5. Place it in the center of a cold oven and turn the temperature to 450 F. Bake for 75 minutes and check for doneness. (The roast should need a little further cooking.)

6. Remove the top bacon strips; they should be nicely browned. Save them to serve with the roast. Push the onion slices aside so that the roast is uncovered; return it to the oven, uncovered, and let it brown for 10 minutes. Remove the venison to a warm place and drape it with a foil tent.

7. Strain the juices accumulated in the pan into a large measuring cup, discarding the bottom bacon strips and pressing down hard on the onion to extract the juices. To degrease the sauce quickly, place the measuring cup in the freezer for 5 minutes. Remove it and carefully spoon off the bacon fat that has risen to the surface. (You should have about 1 cup of liquid. If not, add dry vermouth to make 1 cup.) Pour the juices into a small saucepan and add the reserved mushrooms. Reduce the liquid to ¾ cup over high heat, stirring constantly.

8. Lower the heat, and stir in the flour and water mixture. Stir until the mixture thickens, and let it cook at least 3 minutes to eliminate the flour taste. Add 1 tablespoon of red currant jelly and stir until it dissolves. Remove the pan from the heat and blend in the sour cream. Season with salt and pepper to taste.

9. Bring the roast to the table garnished with the 4 cooked bacon strips. Pass the sauce in a warmed gravy boat, and serve with currant jelly.

DAUBE OF BEEF

Carol Cutler

6 to 8 servings

A *daube* is not just any kind of stew. It has a very specific definition: it is made with meat; it is braised in a stock, generally red wine; it is well-seasoned with herbs and spices; it is cooked slowly in a covered casserole. In France there are pots made just for cooking this oldtime favorite supper dish; fittingly it is called a *daubière*. Clay cookers are an admirable substitute for a true *daubière* since they keep all the ingredients tightly contained in the vessel, sealing in all the flavors and juices. Other meats can be used in the recipe, such as lamb or pork.

2 MEDIUM-SIZED ONIONS, SLICED	1 TEASPOON BASIL
4 CARROTS, SLICED	SALT
¼ POUND CURED HAM OR CANADIAN BACON, CUT IN ½-INCH PIECES	FRESHLY GROUND PEPPER
	1 BAY LEAF
3 POUNDS LEAN STEWING BEEF, CUT IN 2-INCH PIECES	1-POUND CAN OF TOMATOES
	¼ CUP BRANDY
3 CLOVES GARLIC, MINCED	3 CUPS RED WINE
1 TEASPOON THYME	

1. Select a clay cooker that holds about 3 quarts and soak the bottom half in water for 15 minutes.

2. Meanwhile, prepare the vegetables and dice the ham.

3. Put half the beef pieces in the cooker and sprinkle them with half the onions, carrots, ham, garlic, thyme, and basil. Sprinkle very lightly with salt and more generously with pepper. Tuck in a bay leaf.

4. Add half the tomatoes in a layer, first crushing them with your hands as you put them in. Repeat with the remaining beef and other ingredients. Pour in the tomato juice from the can. Pour in the brandy and, finally, the red wine. The liquid should cover about three-quarters of the meat. Marinate for at least 2 hours.

5. Soak the top of the clay cooker in water for 15 minutes.

6. Place a cookie sheet in a cold oven and put the covered cooker on it. Turn the oven to 425 F. and bake for about 1½ hours. Stir the meat pieces once or twice during the cooking.

7. Test the beef for tenderness by piercing it with a small sharp knife. Serve at the table directly from the cooker, and pass steamed potatoes.

SMOKED PORK CHOPS WITH TURNIPS

Elizabeth Colchie

2 to 3 servings

1 POUND VERY SMALL TURNIPS,
   PEELED (THERE SHOULD BE
   ABOUT 8 TO 10; IF TURNIPS ARE
   LARGE, HALVE OR QUARTER THEM)
2 TO 3 SMOKED PORK CHOPS WITH
   BONE, ABOUT ¾- TO 1-INCH THICK
1 SMALL ONION, THINLY SLICED
1 TEASPOON MARJORAM
½ TEASPOON SALT
¼ TEASPOON PEPPER

1. Soak a 2-quart clay cooker in water for 15 minutes.

2. Arrange the turnips, pork and onion in the bottom half of the cooker. Sprinkle over the marjoram, salt and pepper and cover with the top.

3. Place the pot in a cold oven and turn the heat to 400 F. Bake for 20 minutes.

4. Rearrange the chops and turnips so the top vegetables will be on the bottom to absorb some of the meat juices. Cover the pot and cook about 15 minutes longer, or until the turnips are tender.

RACK OF LAMB WITH CORIANDER AND GARLIC

Nathalie Dupree

3 to 4 servings

2 TABLESPOONS CORIANDER SEEDS
4 CLOVES GARLIC
1 TABLESPOON SALT
2 RACKS OF LAMB, 1½ POUND EACH,
   TRIMMED
1 SLICED CARROT
1 SLICED CELERY STALK
PEPPER

1. Soak a 3-quart clay cooker, top and bottom, in water for 15 minutes.

2. Place the coriander seeds between layers of waxed paper and crush them roughly with a rolling pin. With a small knife, chop the garlic and crush it with salt on a board until it is a paste. Rub the garlic and coriander on the lamb.

3. Place the sliced carrot and celery in the bottom of the cooker. Add the two racks of lamb, arranging one with the fat side down, the other with the fat side up, so that both will fit. Pepper them lightly and cover the pot.

4. Place the pot in a cold oven, set the oven at 450 F. and cook for 1 hour and 15 minutes. Uncover the pot for the last 10 minutes, rearranging the lamb so the fat is exposed on both pieces, in order to brown and crisp the skin.

5. Strain the liquid from the pan, discarding the vegetables. Skim off the fat, reheat the liquid and serve. (Optional: You may thicken the liquid with arrow-root or cornstarch if you prefer a thicker sauce.)

Note: This recipe is for those who like their lamb succulent but well done.

SPICED PORK AND CHESTNUT CASSEROLE

Elizabeth Colchie

4 servings

¾ CUP DRIED CHESTNUTS*
1¾ CUPS WATER
1 TEASPOON SUGAR
2¼ POUNDS PORK SHOULDER, CUT IN LARGE CUBES
1 TABLESPOON FLOUR
2 TABLESPOONS PEANUT OIL
1 LARGE PIECE OF PORK RIND (ABOUT 4 INCHES SQUARE) (OPTIONAL)

½ STAR ANISE* "FLOWER" (OR 4 "PETALS")
½ TEASPOON MINCED GARLIC
1 TEASPOON CRUSHED SZECHUAN PEPPERCORNS*
3 TABLESPOONS SOY SAUCE
1 TABLESPOON BROWN SUGAR

1. Soak the chestnuts overnight in water to cover them by at least 4 inches. Drain off the water and remove the husks; there should be about 1½ cups of chestnuts. Combine them in a saucepan with 1 cup of water and the teaspoon of sugar and simmer them, covered, for about 40 minutes or until they are tender (this will vary with the state of dehydration of the chestnuts).

2. Soak a 2-quart clay cooker in water for 15 minutes.

3. Toss the meat with the flour; heat a wok or skillet and pour in the oil. Brown the cubes of meat and place them in the pot.

4. To the chestnuts, add the pork rind, star anise, garlic, pepper, soy sauce, brown sugar and ¾ cup of water and bring them to a boil; pour the mixture over the pork. Cover with the top and put the pot in the oven.

5. Turn the oven to 425 F. and bake for 1½ hours, or until the meat is tender.

*These ingredients are available in Oriental grocery stores.

MARINATED VEAL RIBLETS

Elizabeth Colchie

3 servings

1 TEASPOON GRATED ORANGE RIND
⅔ CUP ORANGE JUICE
2 TEASPOONS SUMMER SAVORY
1 TEASPOON THYME
1 CLOVE GARLIC, SLICED
1 TEASPOON SALT
½ TEASPOON BLACK PEPPER
2 TABLESPOONS OLIVE OIL
3 POUNDS VEAL BREAST (SMALL,
   MEATY RIBLETS, IF POSSIBLE)
1 TABLESPOON FLOUR

1. In a glass or earthenware baking dish or other dish large enough to hold the breast, combine the orange rind and juice, savory, thyme, garlic, salt, black pepper and olive oil and mix them well.

2. Trim the excess fat from the breast and slice it into separate ribs. Turn them to coat in the marinade; cover the dish with plastic wrap and refrigerate for about 12 hours, turning occasionally.

3. Soak a 2-quart clay cooker in water for 15 minutes.

4. Remove the ribs from the marinade, place them in the soaked pot, meat-side up, and sprinkle them evenly with the flour.

5. Place the cooker in the oven and turn the heat to 450 F. Bake for about 1 hour and 15 minutes, or until the ribs are very tender and browned, basting several times with the juices.

ITALIAN POT ROAST (STRACOTTO MALUGANI)

Raymond Sokolov

6 servings

3 POUNDS TOP- OR EYE-ROUND
   OF BEEF
SALT
FRESHLY GROUND PEPPER
¼ TEASPOON GROUND ALLSPICE
1 SMALL ONION, FINELY CHOPPED
1 TABLESPOON OLIVE OIL
1 TABLESPOON BUTTER
1 OR 2 CLOVES GARLIC, FINELY
   CHOPPED

2 BAY LEAVES
½ TEASPOON DRIED SAGE LEAVES,
   CRUMBLED
¼ TEASPOON GRATED NUTMEG
2 CUPS DRY RED WINE
1 CAN (1 POUND 10 OUNCES)
   PEELED ITALIAN TOMATOES
1 CAN (8 OUNCES) TOMATO SAUCE

1. Buy the meat in one solid lean piece and have the butcher tie it up well. Sprinkle all over with salt, pepper and allspice. Let it rest for 15 minutes.

2. Soak a 3-quart clay cooker in water for 15 minutes.

3. In a heavy skillet, sauté the onion in oil and butter. When it begins to brown, add the garlic and let it brown. Then add the meat, bay leaves, sage and nutmeg. Brown the meat on all sides, over high heat. Transfer the meat to the clay pot.

4. Pour the wine into the skillet to deglaze it. Add the tomatoes and their liquid and the tomato sauce. Let the liquid simmer for a few minutes, taste for seasoning and pour it over the meat.

5. Cover the pot and put it in the oven. Turn the heat to 400 F. and let it cook for 2 hours. Uncover the pot and continue cooking for a further ½ hour to reduce and thicken the sauce. Serve with pasta.

LAMB SHANKS WITH DILL SAUCE

Emanuel and Madeline Greenberg

4 servings

4 LAMB SHANKS (3 TO 4 POUNDS) WITH BONES CRACKED
2 CLOVES GARLIC, MINCED
1 LARGE ONION, CHOPPED
¼ CUP CHOPPED PARSLEY
2 TABLESPOONS LEMON JUICE
SALT TO TASTE
PEPPER TO TASTE

½ POUND MUSHROOMS, CUT IN LARGE PIECES
1 CUP DRY WHITE WINE
½ PINT SOUR CREAM, AT ROOM TEMPERATURE
1 TABLESPOON FLOUR
1 TABLESPOON FINELY CHOPPED FRESH DILL

1. Soak a 3-quart clay cooker in water for 15 minutes.

2. Place the shanks in the pot. Combine the garlic, onion, parsley, lemon juice, salt and pepper and spoon it over the meat. Add the mushrooms and pour in the wine.

3. Cover the pot and place it in a cold oven. Set the oven at 400 F. and cook 1½ to 2 hours, or until the meat is tender.

4. Pour the lamb juices into a small saucepan and boil until they are reduced to about ½ cup. Combine the sour cream and flour, stirring until it is smooth. Whisk the cream into the pan juices. Add the dill and simmer over low heat just until the sauce is heated through. Spoon the sauce over the meat.

VEAL IN THE GREEK MANNER

Michael Batterberry

6 to 8 servings

3 POUNDS GOOD STEWING VEAL IN
  LARGE CUBES
½ MEDIUM-SIZED ONION, THINLY
  SLICED
½ JUICY LEMON
1 TABLESPOON GROUND CUMIN
½ TABLESPOON COARSE SALT
FRESHLY GROUND WHITE PEPPER

1. Soak a 4-quart clay cooker in cold water for 15 minutes.

2. Drain the pot and line the bottom and sides with two crisscrossed pieces of buttered parchment paper or aluminum foil.

3. In the parchment nest, layer the veal with the separated onion slices and sprinkle evenly with drops of lemon juice, cumin, salt and pepper.

4. Cover the veal with another piece of buttered parchment or foil and cover the pot.

5. Place the pot in a cold oven and turn the heat to 325 F. Bake for 2 hours and 15 minutes. Test for doneness—the veal should be fork tender—and return it to the oven, if necessary, for another 15 to 30 minutes. Serve it with plain rice, the natural juices and an *avgolemono* sauce.

Avgolemono Sauce:
1 CUP CHICKEN OR VEAL STOCK
1½ TABLESPOONS CORNSTARCH
¼ CUP DRY WHITE WINE
3 EGG YOLKS
JUICE OF ½ LEMON
SALT
FRESHLY GROUND WHITE PEPPER

1. Bring the stock to a simmer. Dissolve the cornstarch in the wine and stir it into the hot stock. Keep stirring until the sauce thickens, approximately 5 minutes.

2. Beat the egg yolks and lemon juice together. Beating constantly, slowly dribble in, a spoonful at a time, about ½ cup of the hot sauce.

3. Pour the egg mixture into the remaining hot sauce, beating constantly. Do not allow it to boil. Season with salt and pepper and additional lemon juice, if needed.

PORK LOIN ROAST WITH SAUERKRAUT

Paul Rubinstein

4 to 6 servings

4 CUPS FRESH SAUERKRAUT
1 LARGE ONION, SLICED VERY THIN
1 TART APPLE, CORED AND SLICED
  (NOT PEELED)
4 STRIPS BACON CUT INTO 1-INCH
  PIECES
1 TEASPOON SUGAR
1 BAY LEAF
3 TO 4 POUNDS BONED PORK LOIN,
  TIED
½ TEASPOON SALT
¼ TEASPOON FRESHLY GROUND
  BLACK PEPPER

1. Soak a 3-quart clay cooker in water for 15 minutes.

2. In the bottom of the clay pot, combine the sauerkraut with its liquid, the sliced onion, apple, bacon pieces, sugar and bay leaf. Toss until it is well mixed.

3. Place the tied pork roast on top of the sauerkraut mixture and sprinkle the meat with salt and pepper.

4. Cover and place the cooker in a cold oven. Set the oven dial at 425 F. and bake for 3 hours.

5. To serve, remove the meat to a warm platter and keep it warm. Remove the sauerkraut mixture with tongs or two slotted spoons and keep it warm in a bowl or vegetable server.

6. Pour the remaining juices into a small saucepan, bring to a simmer, skim off most of the fat, then use the remaining liquid as a gravy.

RABBIT AND PEARL ONIONS (LAGOS STIFADO)

Vilma Liacouras Chantiles

6 servings

Hellenes love to invent words and dishes; they succeed admirably with this dish. *Stifado* is from the Italian word for stew. The Greek version always includes an equal weight of small white onions combined with rabbit or veal. Sometimes another vegetable such as eggplant is used and there are always very spicy seasonings. Flavor improves the second day.

If you use veal in place of the rabbit, it's not necessary to sauté the meat before baking it. Use half the quantity of liquid called for here and reduce the cooking time by 15 minutes.

Continued from preceding page

3 POUNDS RABBIT
½ CUP VINEGAR
1 CUP DRY WHITE WINE
1 ONION, SLICED
1 CARROT, SLICED
1 STALK CELERY, SLICED
1 BAY LEAF
2 SPRIGS PARSLEY
4 PEPPERCORNS

1. Cut the rabbit into serving pieces and place them in a glass or ceramic bowl with all of the other ingredients and let stand for 12 hours at room temperature (if it's not too warm) or for 24 hours in the refrigerator.

⅓ CUP VEGETABLE OIL
1½ CUPS DRY WHITE WINE
1½ CUPS TOMATO PURÉE OR SAUCE
1 LARGE STICK CINNAMON
4 TABLESPOONS WINE VINEGAR
2 CLOVES GARLIC
1½ BAY LEAVES
1 TABLESPOON BROWN SUGAR
SALT
FRESHLY GROUND PEPPER
3 POUNDS WHITE PEARL ONIONS,
   PEELED AND LEFT WHOLE
   (SEE NOTE)

1. Soak a 3-quart clay cooker in cold water for 15 minutes or longer.
2. Dry the rabbit pieces and sauté them in the vegetable oil. Transfer the pieces to the clay cooker, pour out the oil and deglaze the skillet with the wine. Stir the tomato purée, cinnamon, vinegar, garlic, bay leaves and brown sugar into the wine.
3. Salt and pepper the rabbit, add the onions and pour in the wine mixture.
4. Cover the pot, place it in a cold oven, and bake the rabbit at 400 F. for approximately 2 hours.

Note: To prevent the onions from falling apart during the cooking, cut an "X" into the root of each onion before peeling it. Peeling is made much easier if the onions are first immersed in boiling water for 2 minutes.

ITALIAN SHEPHERD'S LAMB STEW
(SPEZZATO D'AGNELLO)

Nicola Zanghi

2 to 3 servings

1½ POUNDS BONELESS LAMB FROM
SHOULDER, LEG OR RUMP, CUT
INTO 1-INCH CUBES
4 SMALL POTATOES, UNPEELED,
CUT INTO ½-INCH CUBES
3 RIBS CELERY, PEELED AND CUT
INTO 1-INCH LENGTHS
3 CARROTS, SPLIT LENGTHWISE
AND CUT INTO 1-INCH LENGTHS
1 LEEK, WHITE PART ONLY, WELL-
WASHED AND CUT INTO 1-INCH
LENGTHS

1½ CUPS SMALL FRESH BUTTON
MUSHROOMS
1 CUP LIGHT DRY RED WINE
¼ CUP WINE VINEGAR
4 TOMATOES, SEEDED AND
COARSELY CUT
1 TABLESPOON JUNIPER BERRIES
½ CUP LAMB OR BEEF STOCK
SALT
PEPPER

1. Soak a 2-quart clay cooker in water for 15 minutes.

2. Place all of the ingredients in the cooker and salt and pepper to taste. Cover, place the pot in the oven and turn the heat to 425 F. Bake for ½ hour.

3. Lower the heat to 375 F. and continue baking for 1 hour longer.

4. Transfer the stew to a serving dish. If you like, pour the accumulated juices into a small saucepan and boil them down until they are the consistency of heavy cream. Pour the sauce over the stew.

Desserts

APPLE-BREAD PUDDING

Joanne Will

6 servings

½ LOAF FRENCH BREAD, CUT INTO
¾-INCH SLICES
4 TABLESPOONS (½ STICK) PLUS
1 TABLESPOON BUTTER,
SOFTENED
3 TART, JUICY APPLES, PARED, CUT
INTO QUARTERS, CORED AND
SLICED CROSSWISE INTO
CHUNKS

GRATED RIND AND JUICE OF 1 LEMON
(ABOUT 3 TABLESPOONS)
½ CUP PACKED BROWN SUGAR
1 TEASPOON CINNAMON
½ CUP GOLDEN RAISINS
⅓ CUP APPLE JUICE OR CIDER
(IF NECESSARY)

1. Soak a 2-quart clay cooker in water for 15 minutes.

2. Spread both sides of the French bread with 4 tablespoons of butter. Cut it into chunks. You should have about 1 quart of bread chunks.

3. Butter the bottom of the clay pot with the remaining tablespoon of butter. Put half the bread cubes in the pot.

4. Mix the apples with the grated rind, lemon juice, brown sugar, cinnamon and raisins. Spoon the mixture over the bread in the clay cooker. Top with the remaining bread cubes.

5. Cover the pot and put it in the center of a cold oven. Set the temperature to 425 F. and bake 45 to 50 minutes.

6. Serve the pudding warm with half-and-half, whipped cream, ice cream, or lemon-flavored yogurt.

Note: If the apples do not seem to be juicy, drizzle the ingredients with ⅓ cup apple juice or apple cider before baking.

BAKED APPLES

Maurice Moore-Betty

4 servings

4 TABLESPOONS (½ STICK)
  SOFTENED BUTTER
4 TABLESPOONS BROWN SUGAR
4 TABLESPOONS SEEDLESS RAISINS,
  CHOPPED
PINCH NUTMEG
PINCH CINNAMON
2 TABLESPOONS DARK RUM
2 TABLESPOONS LEMON JUICE
4 GRANNY SMITH OR MACKINTOSH
  APPLES

1. Soak a 2-quart clay cooker in cold water for 15 minutes.

2. Mix the first five ingredients together with a wooden spoon in a bowl. Add the rum and lemon juice gradually until they are absorbed.

3. Core the apples and peel the skin from the top half of each apple.

4. Stand the apples in the pot. Pack the cored holes tightly with the butter-raisin mixture. Cover with the other half of the clay pot. Stand it on a baking sheet in a cold oven. Set the temperature control at 450 F. and bake the apples for 40 minutes.

5. Test with a fork prong for doneness; apples vary and 40 minutes is only a guide.

BAKED CHOCOLATE PUDDING

Paul Rubinstein

6 servings

6 EGGS, SEPARATED
1 CUP GRANULATED SUGAR
1 CUP GRATED SEMI-SWEET
  CHOCOLATE
3 TABLESPOONS FINE GRAHAM
  CRACKER CRUMBS
1¼ TEASPOONS DOUBLE-ACTING
  BAKING POWDER

1 TEASPOON VANILLA EXTRACT
½ CUP CHOPPED ALMONDS
⅛ TEASPOON SALT
1 TABLESPOON BUTTER
2 TABLESPOONS POWDERED
  CONFECTIONERS' SUGAR
1 PINT (2 CUPS) HEAVY CREAM,
  WELL CHILLED

1. Soak a 3-quart cooker in water for 30 minutes.

2. Beat the egg yolks in the large bowl of an electric mixer until pale yellow and fluffy, then continue beating and add the granulated sugar, a little at a time, until all of it is incorporated.

Continued from preceding page

3. Turn the mixer to the slowest speed and mix in the grated chocolate, graham cracker crumbs, baking powder, vanilla extract and almonds.

4. Separately, beat the egg whites with the salt until they form soft peaks. Fold them gently but thoroughly into the chocolate mixture.

5. Coat the bottom of the clay cooker with the butter, and dust with powdered sugar, discarding any excess that does not adhere to the butter.

6. Turn the batter into the cooker, cover and place it in a cold oven. Turn the oven control to 375 F. and bake for 1¾ hours.

7. Serve the pudding directly from the bowl of the clay cooker, spooning hot pudding onto dessert plates, with chilled cream in a pitcher to accompany it. Do not attempt to unmold the entire pudding onto a serving platter.

STEAMED MARMALADE PUDDING WITH CUSTARD SAUCE

Nan Mabon

6 servings

GRAND MARNIER CUSTARD SAUCE
   (SEE BELOW)
8 TABLESPOONS (1 STICK) BUTTER
   (PREFERABLY UNSALTED)
¾ CUP DARK BROWN SUGAR
2 LARGE EGGS
4 TABLESPOONS MARMALADE
GRATED RIND OF 1 MEDIUM-SIZED
   ORANGE
1 TEASPOON BAKING SODA
1 CUP FLOUR
OPTIONAL GARNISH: 6 GLACÉED
   ORANGE SLICES

1. Soak a clay pot in water for 15 minutes.

2. Beat the butter until light and creamy, then beat in the brown sugar.

3. Add the eggs, one at a time, then stir in the marmalade and the grated rind.

4. Sift the soda and flour directly into the mixing bowl, stirring to blend.

5. Generously butter a 1-quart soufflé dish or bowl that will fit into the clay pot. If the pot is too small to accommodate the dish, completely line the bottom of the pot with buttered foil.

6. Scrape the batter into the soufflé dish and cover the top with another sheet of foil. If you are using only the clay pot, pour the batter into the center.

7. Put the cover in place and set the pot in the oven. Set the temperature to 350 F. and bake for 1½ hours.

8. When ready to serve, run a knife around the edge and turn out onto a serving platter. Surround the pudding with glacéed orange slices and pass the sauce separately.

   Note: If you are not serving the pudding immediately, remove it from the oven and keep it in the covered pot until you are ready. It should stay warm for an hour.

Grand Marnier Custard Sauce:
3 EGG YOLKS
1½ CUPS MILK
1 VANILLA POD OR ½ TEASPOON
   VANILLA
3 TABLESPOONS SUGAR
2 TABLESPOONS GRAND MARNIER

1. Whisk the yolks in a small mixing bowl until they are light and creamy.

2. Scald the milk in an enameled pan with the vanilla pod and the sugar.

3. Pour the hot milk onto the yolks, remove the pod and return yolks and milk to the pan. Stir over moderate heat until the liquid coats the back of a spoon. Cool and stir in the Grand Marnier. Strain it into a serving container.

EDITORS

Arnold Goldman
Barbara Spiegel
Lyn Stallworth

EDITORIAL ASSISTANT

Christopher Carter

EDITORIAL CONSULTANTS

Wendy Afton Rieder
Kate Slate

CONTRIBUTORS

Introduction by Lyn Stallworth

Michael Batterberry, author of several books on food, art and social history, is also a painter, and is editor and food critic for a number of national magazines. He has taught at James Beard's cooking classes in New York and many of his original recipes have appeared in *House & Garden, House Beautiful* and *Harper's Bazaar.*

Paula J. Buchholz is the regional co-ordinator for the National Culinary Apprenticeship Program. She has been a food writer for the *Detroit Free Press* and for the *San Francisco Examiner.*

Giuliano Bugialli, author of *The Fine Art of Italian Cooking,* is co-founder and teacher of Cooking in Florence, a program conducted in Italy. He also has a cooking school in New York.

Vilma Liacouras Chantiles, author of *The Food of Greece,* writes a food and consumer column for the *Scarsdale* (New York) *Inquirer* and a monthly food column for the *Athenian Magazine* (Athens, Greece).

Ruth Ellen Church, a syndicated wine columnist for the *Chicago Tribune,* had been food editor for that newspaper for more than thirty years when she recently retired. The author of seven cookbooks, her most recent book is *Entertaining with Wine.* Mrs. Church's *Wines and Cheeses of the Midwest* will be published in the fall of 1977.

Elizabeth Colchie is a noted food consultant who has done extensive recipe development and testing as well as research into the history of foods and cookery. She was on the editorial staff of *The Cooks' Catalogue* and has written numerous articles for such magazines as *Gourmet, House & Garden* and *Family Circle.*

Isabel S. Cornell, a home economist, was Associate Editor for the revised edition of *Woman's Day Encyclopedia of Cookery* and Special Projects Editor for the revised edition of *Woman's Day Collector's Cook Book.* While on the Woman's Day staff, she selected, tested and judged for their recipe contests.

Carol Cutler, who has been a food columnist for the *Washington Post,* is a graduate of the Cordon Bleu and L'École des Trois Gourmands in Paris. She is the author of *Haute Cuisine for Your Heart's Delight* and *The Six-Minute Soufflé and Other Culinary Delights.* She has also written for *House & Garden, American Home* and *Harper's Bazaar.*

Nathalie Dupree has been Director of Rich's Cooking School in Atlanta, Georgia, since it opened in September, 1975. She has an Advanced Certificate from the London Cordon Bleu and has owned restaurants in Spain and Georgia.

Florence Fabricant is a free-lance writer, reporting on restaurants and food for *The New York Times, New York* magazine and other publications. She was on the staff of *The Cooks' Catalogue* and editor of the paperback edition.

Emanuel and Madeline Greenberg co-authored *Whiskey in the Kitchen* and are consultants to the food and beverage industry. Emanuel, a home economist, is a regular contributor to the food columns of *Playboy* magazine.

Diana Kennedy, the leading authority on the food of Mexico, is the author of *The Cuisines of Mexico* and *The Tortilla Book.*

Carole Lalli is a contributing editor to *New West* magazine and its restaurant reviewer. She formerly ran a catering business in New York.

Nan Mabon, a free-lance food writer and cooking teacher in New York City, is also the cook for a private executive dining room on Wall Street. She studied at the Cordon Bleu in London.

Maurice Moore-Betty, owner-operator of The Civilized Art Cooking School, food consultant and restaurateur, is author of *Cooking for Occasions, The Maurice Moore-Betty Cooking School Book of Fine Cooking* and *The Civilized Art of Salad Making.*

Jane Moulton, a food writer for the *Plain Dealer* in Cleveland, took her degree in foods and nutrition. As well as reporting on culinary matters and reviewing food-related books for the *Plain Dealer,* she has worked in recipe development, public relations and catering.

Paul Rubinstein is the author of *Feasts for Two, The Night Before Cookbook* and *Feasts for Twelve (or More).* He is a stockbroker and the son of pianist Artur Rubinstein.

Raymond Sokolov, author of *The Saucier's Apprentice,* is a free-lance writer with a particular interest in food.

Lyn Stallworth was associated with Time-Life *Foods of the World* series and has written a food column for *Viva* magazine.

Michael Tong is Managing Director of three of the finest Chinese restaurants in New York: Shun Lee Dynasty, Shun Lee Palace and Hunam.

Joanne Will is food editor of the *Chicago Tribune* and a member of three Chicago wine and food societies.

Nicola Zanghi is the owner-chef of Restaurant Zanghi in Glen Cove, New York. He started his apprenticeship under his father at the age of thirteen, and is a graduate of two culinary colleges. He is an instructor at the Cordon Bleu school in New York City.